Human Services and Native Americans

DuBray

THOMSON
⎯⎯⎯ ✳ ⎯⎯⎯™
WADSWORTH

Australia · Canada · Mexico · Singapore · Spain · United Kingdom · United States

Human Services and Native Americans
DuBray

Executive Editors:
Michele Baird, Maureen Staudt &
Michael Stranz

Project Development Manager:
Linda deStefano

Sr. Marketing Coordinators:
Lindsay Annett and Sara Mercurio

Production/Manufacturing Manager:
Donna M. Brown

Production Editorial Manager:
Dan Plofchan

Pre-Media Services Supervisor:
Becki Walker

Rights and Permissions Specialists:
Kalina Hintz and Bahman Naraghi

Cover Image
Getty Images*

The Adaptable Courseware Program
consists of products and additions to
existing Thomson products that are
produced from camera-ready copy.
Peer review, class testing, and
accuracy are primarily the responsibility
of the author(s).

For more information, please contact
Thomson Custom Solutions, 5191
Natorp Boulevard, Mason, OH 45040.
Or you can visit our Internet site at
www.thomsoncustom.com

For permission to use material from this
text or product, contact us by:
Tel (800) 730-2214
Fax (800) 730 2215
www.thomsonrights.com

ISBN-13: 978-0-314-01356-9
ISBN-10: 0-314-01356-3

International Divisions List

Asia (Including India):
Thomson Learning
(a division of Thomson Asia Pte Ltd)
5 Shenton Way #01-01
UIC Building
Singapore 068808
Tel: (65) 6410-1200
Fax: (65) 6410-1208

Australia/New Zealand:
Thomson Learning Australia
102 Dodds Street
Southbank, Victoria 3006
Australia

Latin America:
Thomson Learning
Seneca 53
Colonia Polano
11560 Mexico, D.F., Mexico
Tel (525) 281-2906
Fax (525) 281-2656

Canada:
Thomson Nelson
1120 Birchmount Road
Toronto, Ontario
Canada M1K 5G4
Tel (416) 752-9100
Fax (416) 752-8102

UK/Europe/Middle East/Africa:
Thomson Learning
High Holborn House
50-51 Bedford Row
London, WC1R 4LS
United Kingdom
Tel 44 (020) 7067-2500
Fax 44 (020) 7067-2600

Spain (Includes Portugal):
Thomson Paraninfo
Calle Magallanes 25
28015 Madrid
España
Tel 34 (0)91 446-3350
Fax 34 (0)91 445-6218

DEDICATION

To my daughter Yvonne whose beauty
and compassion graced this place all
too briefly, and to my children,
David, Les, Diane and my grandchildren,
Angela, Joseph and Peter.

CONTENTS

PREFACE

Cultural Awareness is a first step in preparing human service workers to relate more effectively with clients from communities that are culturally different from their own.

This book addresses two needs: (1) the need for human service workers to develop and deliver culturally relevant services, and (2) the need for educational institutions, which prepare human service workers, to provide curricula which is currently relevant.

The interests of minority clients such as American Indians, are poorly represented in the curricula of schools of psychology, psychiatry, social work and nursing and in the daily practices of many social service agencies.

The holistic nature of the American Indian culture and philosophy is complex, but it provides a comprehensive design for living even in our modern world of technology and materialism. The American Indian philosophy has much to contribute to methods of intervention in the human services as well as providing an alternative lifestyle to those willing to examine and experience a paradigm shift.

Cultural variation is one of the most enduring characteristics of all humans. The melting pot theory of cultural blindness still pervades most institutions of higher learning in spite of the efforts of many educators to point out its deficiencies. It is expedient to program developers and service deliverers to view all people as the same under the skin. This simplistic approach looks economical on paper but the cost is borne by those ethnic minority clients who are deprived of culturally relevant services. A similar predicament exists in the cost borne by conscientious human service workers who are aware that the models do not work but are ill equipped to know what is appropriate or relevant.

"Observations of the decline of Western civilization are found everywhere in twentieth-century literature. What we are witnessing is the struggle of both Indian and non-Indian to find answers to their respective and dissimilar situations. This search has led to similar conclusions and attitudes-a variety of attempts to regain contact with the roots of traditions which, viewed by modern day thinkers as old-fashioned and obsolete, have almost slipped into oblivion. It is surprising that the traditions and sacred ways of American Indians have to a large extent prevailed despite the overwhelming efforts of the dominant society to obliterate them. For many urban as well as reservation Indians, that ancient tradition continues to provide a sense of alternative values which lends wholeness to the otherwise shattered experience of the materialistic twentieth-century life...

It is not surprising that non-Indians, especially young people, are turning to native peoples and their viable traditions for possible alternatives to the shaken and collapsing values of their own societies (Highwater, 1981, p 202-203).

The hope is that this dual search on the part of Indian and non-Indian will lead to a true and open dialogue through which neither will attempt to imitate the other, but where each may ultimately regain and reaffirm the sacred dimensions of their own respective traditions (Brown, 1969).

An in depth study of the life cycle will show that in terms of conscious dedication to human relationships that are both affective and effective, the American Indian is far ahead of Western societies. The American Indian strives at every stage of life, from infancy to death for order and balance within his/her cosmos; playing and worship are as important as working. Whether at home or at work, life is governed by a social consciousness which remains pervasive until death. Because of that social consciousness each individual is a person of worth and intrinsic value, important to society from the day of birth to the day of death. This social consciousness is based upon spiritualism and is the highest form of political consciousness.

One of the most important concepts in the American Indian perspective is that society is seen as an integrated whole, not as the sum total of a number of distinct parts. A necessary technique for analytical purposes (for the Western mind) is to study the areas of domestic life, economic life, political life and spiritual life. As we observe these areas of American Indian life we realize that a basic philosophy and value orientation emerges in four categories: activity, relationships, time and one's relationship to nature.

The following chapters are an exploration of American Indian values and philosophy as they relate to the domestic, economic, political and spiritual life of a great and humble people. Based upon an understanding of common cultural values of American Indian populations, social workers and other human service workers will be in a more knowledgeable position to provide culturally sensitive mental health, health and other human services to this population.

American Indians are at differing levels of assimilation. Presently most of the tribes have their own governments, manage their own health programs, operate a variety of businesses, manage multi-million dollar budgets, operate their own schools and colleges and yet have a distinct tribal identity. Value studies involving most of the major tribes reveal a core of basic values that are in conflict with the values of the dominant Anglo-American population. In addition social policies for this population are unique, as tribes are recognized as sovereign nations with their own tribal courts, laws and jurisdictional powers. It is important to note the differences between American Indians and other oppressed populations.

REFERENCES

Brown, Joseph E. (1969). The Persistence of Essential Values among North American Plains Indians in Human Services for Cultural Minorities, University Park Press.

Highwater, Jamake (1981). The Primal Mind: Vision and Reality in Indian America, New York, Harper & Row.

A NOTE OF APPRECIATION

This book, while in the making, served as the basis of many lectures to students preparing for a lifetime of human services. Francis Purcell helped me conceptualize and operationalize the methodology of culturally sensitive interventions with American Indian clients. Margaret Eisenbise provided bibliographical assistance in the development of the three bibliographies on Human Behavior, Practice and Social Policy with American Indians. Dan O'Neill, Joan Avis, Frances Hsu and Rogelio Reyes at the University of San Francisco nurtured my interest in researching cultural values of American Indian human service workers. John Erlich at California State University, Sacramento and Tom LaMarre of West Publishing Company provided the encouragement to meet the challenge and complete the manuscript. Some of the chapters were originally developed when I was on the faculty at San Francisco State University some eight years ago. These works have been rewritten and updated to reflect my own evolution as a clinician and educator in the Human Services field. Perhaps my greatest inspiration has come from the thousands of students I have had the privilege of knowing and with whom I shared my American Indian heritage. But most of all I owe the greater part of this work to my Lakota parents who sacrificed their culture with great humility in order that their children might survive in the "white man's world". They would have wanted the truth to be passed on to the generations of the future and for the wounded healers to be healed.

Wynne Hanson DuBray
Lakota

Cover design by Yvonne Leslie Hanson, Lakota Graphic Artist

THE AUTHOR

Wynne Hanson DuBray is an Associate Professor at California State University, Sacramento and a Licensed Clinical Social Worker in private practice in Sacramento, California. She holds a B.A. degree from San Francisco State University, a MSW degree from San Francisco State University and a Doctorate in Psychology from the University of San Francisco.

DuBray has taught at the University of California, Berkeley, San Francisco State University, Los Medanos College in Pittsburgh, California and has lectured extensively throughout North America. She has published numerous articles in professional journals and is a popular workshop presenter.

1. OVERVIEW FROM THE NINETIES

The white man made us many promises, but he kept only one, he promised he would take the land, and he took it...

Lakota Elder

When Columbus landed on North American shores he was met by a people with a very different set of values from those possessed by Europeans. American Indians had lived for thousands of years in a communal type of society. Everything, including the land was shared with all living things. The Native people were known for their generosity and hospitality. Perhaps from a materialistic perspective, this has been the one factor that has led to the most extreme oppression, destruction and extermination of indigenous people in recorded history.

Most Americans are illiterate when it comes to knowledge about American Indian tribes since genocidal practices of the United States government is usually not acknowledge by American historians nor is the true history of American Indians even taught by so called scholars in the classrooms of American Colleges and Universities today. Some faculty avoid discussions on the oppression of American Indians because it is not popular with some Anglo American students who make up the majority of students in our classrooms today (Effman and Moore, 1992).

Some of the best kept secrets about American Indians are the many contributions American Indians have made to American society. American Indians transformed the philosophy of Anglo American colonialists. Indian societies have always had a deep respect for individual liberty. American Indians helped the Europeans to recognize the relevance of individual liberty in the new political order (that they would create) in the development of the Constitution and the Bill of Rights. It is paradoxical that the drafters of the Constitution then proceeded to deprive American Indians of individual freedom and justice (reserved for themselves) and very little has changed for American Indians since.

Benjamin Franklin advocated that the new American government incorporate many of the same features as the government of the Iroquois Indians (Wilson, 1959, p. 46). Speaking to the Albany Congress in 1754, Franklin called on the delegates of the various English colonies to unite and emulate the Iroquois League, a call that was not heeded until the Constitution was written three decades later (Hecht, 1980, p. 71). The Founding Fathers finally adopted some of the essential features of the Iroquois League. The Iroquois League united five principal Indian nations-the Mohawk, Onondaga, Seneca, Oneida and Cayuga. Each of these nations had a council composed of delegates called sachems who were elected by the (tribes of that) nation. In addition to the individual councils of each separate (tribal) nation, the sachems of the six nations discussed issues of common concern. Charles Thomson, secretary of the Continental Congress spent many months studying the Indians and their way of life and was adopted as a member of the Delaware tribe. Thomson wrote at length on Indian social and political institutions. One of the most important characteristics of the Iroquois League was its ability to expand as needed. In a radical break with Old World tradition, the US government emulated the Iroquois tradition of admitting new states as members rather than keeping them as colonies. As the west became a series of territories and then states, the US government through the Congressional Resolution of 1780, the Land Ordinances of 1784 and 1785 accepted these territories as states and codified Indian practice into American law.

American Indians have also made major contributions to modern medicine, agriculture, art, literature, architecture, ecology and foods. Some 60 percent of the foods eaten in the world today were first harvested by the American Indians (Weatherford, 1988).

There has been considerable legal and legislative efforts by the federal government to destroy sovereignty and this continues today. American Indians were denied religious freedom and within the last 5 years several decisions have been handed down by the supreme court to continue that denial. In spite of the federal policies of forced assimilation through the boarding school era and the efforts to destroy American Indian culture over the last two hundred years, American Indians have maintained their tribal identities and show no interest in giving up their identities.

At the time of the arrival of Columbus on North America the population of American Indians was estimated at somewhere between 20 million and 60 million depending upon which historian you are quoting. Today there are approximately 2 million American Indians living in the United States according to the 1990 census. These 2 million people represent over 200 tribes, with many languages and diverse customs and traditions. (A list of states and American Indian populations is included in this section).

Because of the unique historical, political and demographic status of American Indians, it is paramount that social policies effecting this population be fair and just. American Indians are sovereign nations and the United States is legally bound by treaties with these sovereign nations. These policies and treaty rights cannot be compared with what is equal in relation to other racial/ethnic groups in the United States today.

Obligations to provide American Indians with health care, education, and social welfare are included in these treaties between Indian tribes and the United States government. Yet, questions of eligibility and jurisdictional issues continue to prevent Indian people from receiving adequate health care. Though many of the major health problems of American Indians have decreased by 70 percent since federal responsibility for the health care was transferred to the U.S. Public Health Service in 1954, Indians still suffer from high rates of diabetes, hypertension, alcoholism, advanced liver disease and fetal alcohol syndrome. Life expectancy for American Indians is six years less than that of any other minority group in America (Green and Tonnesen, 1991).

The percentage of American Indians who graduated from high school increased from 51 percent in 1970 to 60 percent in 1980. American Indian enrollments in colleges and universities across the United States increased from 76,000 in 1976 to 90,000 in 1986 (Green and Tonnesen, 1991).

The current U.S. policy toward American Indians has come to be known as one of self-determination. Indian gaming is presently the most effective economic program on reservations throughout the country. Tribes report moving from 90% unemployment to full employment in a matter of months after opening gaming establishments. It will be interesting to see whether Congress protects the interests of Indian tribes in the controversy over gaming or yields to owners of high stakes gaming establishments primarily operating in New Jersey and Nevada. It is possible that American Indians will continue to be deprived of true economic independence as penance for the defeat of General Custer at the Battle of the Little Big Horn.

1990 POPULATION COUNT

The population counts of American Indian, Eskimo and Aleut for the 50 states and the District of Columbia are listed by ranking order:

Rank	State	Population	% of State
1	Oklahoma	252,420	8.0
2	California	242,164	0.8
3	Arizona	203,527	5.6
4	New Mexico	134,355	8.9
5	Alaska	85,698	15.6
6	Washington	81,483	1.7
7	North Carolina	80,155	1.2
8	Texas	65,877	0.4
9	New York	62,651	0.3
10	Michigan	55,638	0.6
11	South Dakota	50,575	7.3
12	Minnesota	49,909	1.1
13	Montana	47,679	6.0
14	Wisconsin	39,387	0.8
15	Oregon	38,496	1.4
16	Florida	36,335	0.3
17	Colorado	27,776	0.8
18	North Dakota	25,917	4.1
19	Utah	24,283	1.4
20	Kansas	21,965	0.9
21	Illinois	21,836	0.2
22	Ohio	20.358	0.2
23	Missouri	19,835	0.4
24	Nevada	19,637	1.6
25	Louisiana	18,541	0.4
26	Alabama	16,506	0.4
27	Virginia	15,282	0.2
28	New Jersey	14,970	0.2
29	Pennsylvania	14,733	0.1
30	Idaho	13,780	1.4
31	Georgia	13,348	0.2
32	Maryland	12,972	0.3

33	Arkansas	12,733	0.5
34	Indiana	12,720	0.2
35	Nebraska	12,410	0.8
36	Massachusetts	12,241	0.2
37	Tennessee	10,039	0.2
38	Wyoming	9,479	2.1
39	Mississippi	8,525	0.3
40	South Carolina	8,246	0.2
41	Iowa	7,349	0.3
42	Connecticut	6,654	0.2
43	Maine	5,998	0.5
44	Kentucky	5,769	0.4
45	Hawaii	5,099	0.5
46	Rhode Island	4,071	0.4
47	West Virginia	2,458	0.1
48	New Hampshire	2,134	0.2
49	Delaware	2,019	0.3
50	Vermont	1,696	0.3
51	District of Columbia	1,466	0.2

*The population counts are subject to possible correction for undercount or overcount. The United States Department of Commerce is considering whether to correct these counts. Total: 1,959,094.

REFERENCES

Effman, J. and Moore, J. (personal communication, May 19, 1992).

Green, Donald E., & Tonnesen, Thomas V., (1991) <u>American Indian: Social Justice and Public Policy</u>, University of Wisconsin System, Milwaukee, WI.

Hecht, Robert A. (1980) <u>Continents in Collision</u>. Washington, D.C.: University Press of America.

Weatherford, Jack (1988) <u>Indian Givers</u>, Ballantine Books, New York.

Wilson, Edmund (1959) <u>Apologies to the Iroquois</u>. New York: Farrar, Straus & Giroux.

2. SOCIAL WELFARE POLICY
AND AMERICAN INDIAN POPULATIONS

Introduction

Even a casual review of the literature used by instructors in schools of social work who teach social welfare services and policy will reveal a paucity of material pertaining to American Indians. It is the purpose of this text to provide schools of social work and their teachers a central core of information concerning the policy and provisions of laws that affect American Indians.

All social work students ought to be exposed to this information and the reasons for its existence. The core information which has been selected is not exhaustive, but it is essential.

Included in this section:
  A. Historical Overview
  B. The Bureau of Indian Affairs
  C. Federal Assistance

A. Historical Overview

In order to understand social policies which apply to American <u>Indians</u> one must understand their unique relationship with the federal government.

During the 17th century the United States government signed numerous treaties with the Indian tribes of North America. Each of these tribes was recognized as sovereign nations. These treaties covered many aspects of social welfare for Indians.

Beginning in 1830 the United States Congress decided to discontinue making treaties and began to <u>remove</u> Indians from their lands by force, passing the Indian Removal Act. It then became government policy to set aside barren land as reservations for Indians.

The reservation period has been maintained since 1850 with approximately half of all Indians presently living on reservations.

In 1887 the federal government broke up tribal holdings (reservation land) by dividing them up into small parcels and distributing them to individual Indians. This plan was not productive for most tribes and the process was later reversed by the passage of the Indian reorganization act.

The Johnson O'Malley Act, passed in 1934, allowed the federal government to contract with states and other agencies to deliver special services to Indians, such as education.

From 1953-1968 the federal government attempted to terminate the special trust relationships with tribes. These were difficult years for Indians as most were not yet ready to assume full responsibility for themselves in a culture now dominated by Europeans.

President Johnson with House Concurrent Resolution 108 called for an official end of tribal termination policy and the need to support tribal "self-determination without termination."

Following the policy reversal in 1968, P.L. 93-638, the Indian Self-Determination and Educational Assistance Act was signed into law in 1975. The Indian Child Welfare Act passed in 1978 further commits federal policy to the support of self-determination without termination.

It is sad but true that many social workers attempting to perform an advocate role are not fully aware of the implications of this special tribal-federal relationship upon which important decisions should be based.

It is also important to note that in most legal clashes between tribes and the federal government the tribes are seldom demanding new or additional rights or favors. The issues almost always focus upon whether or not the federal government will uphold what it has already promised itself to do by treaties.

It is in many instances the social worker (informed about Indian law) who plays a vital role in communicating this reality to individuals and groups in the community.

The balance of material in this section explains in greater detail specific policies applicable to Indians. It is hoped that the student will do additional reading from the comprehensive bibliography on social policy and American Indians included in this text.

B. The Bureau of Indian Affairs

At one time the Bureau of Indian Affairs (BIA) was the only federal agency with more than minimal contact with Indians. But now the BIA, an agency of the Department of the Interior, has been joined by the Departments of Health and Human Services (HHS), Housing and Urban Development (HUD), Commerce, and others.

The Office of the Solicitor, which is the general counsel for the Interior Department, handles most of the Indian legal issues within the government. Responsibility is focused on the Associate Solicitor for Indian Affairs, who has a staff of some 20 Indian law specialists in Washington. The Associate Solicitor issues opinions which resolve many legal questions on the reservations, prepares litigation for the government on behalf of the Indians, and generally advocates Indian interests within the Department of Interior.

For its first 100 years, the BIA was the municipal government on the reservations by building road, managing the land, operating the court systems and providing social services. Changes came about in the 1930's when the programs of the New Deal brought other agencies to the reservations including the Social Security Act of 1935. The Great Society of the 1960's also dispersed additional federal programs in Indian Country.

The tribes are rivals of the BIA and have a love/hate relationship with the agency. Though critical of BIA policies, tribes are quick to avoid total dismantlement as that could lead to termination of the land base and reservation programs. The BIA under the leadership of Dr. Eddie Brown, a former social work professor from Arizona State University, is presently undergoing restructuring. The tribes have given input into the new structure which would give tribes more control over their economic development and mineral leases.

The child welfare services for the Indian populations are administered by the BIA and the Indian Child Welfare Act of 1978 is provided in this text under the chapter on child welfare.

As trustee of the Indian, the BIA is a pervasive presence in the Indian world. The BIA jurisdiction covers more than 50 millions acres which belong to the Indians. This agency is both an economic and political force. The BIA agency serves as social worker, teacher, realtor, banker, employer contract office, chamber of commerce, highway authority, housing authority, police department, conservation service, water works, telephone company, planning office land developer, guardian protector and spokesman. Based in Washington, DC, the agency has regional offices with over 16,000 employees. It could be said that Indians may not do anything on the reservation unless it is specifically permitted by the government.

C. Federal Assistance Available to American Indians

Federal assistance is available to American Indians by way of advisory services, counseling, use of property, facilities, and equipment; and educational grants and scholarships. The following list includes some of the more popular programs.:

Indian Business Enterprise Development
Indian Loans--Economic Development
Indian Tribea and Tribal Corporation Loans
Indian Arts and Crafts Development
Health Professions Preparatory Scholarship Program
Health Professions Scholarship Program
Indian Education--Colleges and Universities
Indian Education--Fellowships for Indian Students
Indian Education--Special Programs and Projects
Employment and Training--Indian Management Grants
Indian Health Services--Health Management Grants
Indian Loans--Claims Assistance (Expert Witness)
Indian Social Service--Child Welfare Assistance
Foster Grandparent Program
Indian Social Services--General Assistance
Native American Programs
Social Services Research and Demonstration
Medicare Hospital Insurance
Medicare--Supplementary Medical Insurance
Social Security--Disability Insurance
Social Security--Retirement Insurance
Social Security--Survivors Insurance
Supplementary Security Income
Mini-Grant Program
Training and Technical Assistance--Tribal Governments

Indian Health Service

The Indian Health Service, a branch of the Public Health Service within Health and Human Services provides comprehensive health services for federally recognized tribal members. Services include dental, medical, mental health, nursing, alcohol counseling, environmental health and health education.

Some tribes operate their health programs under contract with the Indian Health Service through PL 93-638 legislation. Other hospitals and clinics are operated directly by the Indian Health Service. The tribes in California operate their own comprehensive health programs and utilize local hospitals for inpatient needs.

Since 1955, the Indian Health Service, under the Public Health Service, has had the responsibility for providing comprehensive health services to American Indian and Alaska Native people in order to elevate their health status to the highest possible level. The mission of the IHS is to ensure the equity, availability and accessibility of a comprehensive high quality health care delivery system providing maximum involvement of American Indians and Alaska Natives in defining their health needs, setting priorities for their local areas, and managing and controlling their health program. Federal Indian health services are based on the laws which the Congress has passed pursuant to its authority to regulate commerce with the Indian Nations as explicitly specified in the Constitution and in other pertinent authorities.

The Indian Health program became a primary responsibility of the PHS under PL 83-568, the Transfer Act, on August 5, 1954. This Act provided "that all functions, responsibilities, authorities, and duties...relating to the maintenance and operation of hospital and health facilities for Indians, and the conservation of Indian health...shall be administered by the Surgeon General of the United States Public Health Service."

The IHS goal is to elevate the health status of American Indians and Alaska Natives to the highest level possible with limited funding. The IHS also acts as the principal Federal health advocate for Indian people by assuring they have knowledge of and access to all Federal, State, and local health programs they are entitled to as American citizens. It is also the responsibility of the IHS to work with these programs so they will be cognizant of entitlements of Indian people.

The IHS has carried out its responsibilities through developing and operating a health services delivery system designed to provide a broad-spectrum program of preventive, curative, rehabilitative and environmental services. This system integrates health services delivered directly through IHS facilities and staff on the one hand, with those purchased by IHS through contractual arrangements on the other, taking into account other health resources to which the Indians have access. Tribes are also actively involved in program implementation.

The 1975 Indian Self-Determination Act PL 93-638 as amended, builds upon IHS policy by giving Tribes the option of manning and managing IHS programs in their communities, and provides for funding for improvement of Tribal capability to contract under the Act. The 1976 Indian Health Care Improvement Act PL 94-437, as amended was intended to elevate the health status of American Indians and Alaska Natives to a level equal to that of the general population through a program of authorized higher resource levels in the IHS budget. Appropriated resources were used to expand health services, build and renovate medical facilities, and step up the construction of safe drinking water and sanitary disposal facilities. It also established programs designed to increase the number of Indian health professionals for Indian needs and to improve health care for Indian people living in urban areas.

The leading cause of death for American Indians and Alaska Natives residing in the Reservation States (1986-1988) was "diseases of the heart" followed by "accidents." However the cause of death rankings differ by sex. For Indian males the top two causes were also "diseases of the heart" and "accidents". For Indian females, the tope two causes were "diseases of the heart" and "malignant neoplasms" (the same as for the total US All Races population in 1987).

In 1988, the Indian (Reservation State) age-adjusted mortality rates for the following causes were considerably higher than those for the US All Races population:
1) alcoholism-438 percent greater
2) tuberculosis-400 percent greater
3) diabetes mellitus-155 percent greater
4) accidents-131 percent greater
5) homicide-57 percent greater
6) pneumonia and influenza-32 percent greater
7) suicides-27 percent greater

For the period 1979-1981, the life expectancy at birth for American Indians and Alaska Natives residing in the Reservation States was 71.1 years (67.1 years for males 75.1 years for females), up 6.0 years from 1969-71. Despite these gains, life expectancy at birth for Indians lagged behind that for the US White population in 1980 (74.4 years for both sexes, 70.7 years for males, and 78.1 years for females).

There are 33 Reservation States as of October 1, 1990. The Reservation States are:

Alabama	Maine	North Dakota
Alaska	Massachusetts	Oklahoma
Arizona	Michigan	Oregon
California	Minnesota	Pennsylvania
Colorado	Mississippi	Rhode Island
Connecticut	Montana	South Dakota
Florida	Nebraska	Texas
Idaho	Nevada	Utah
Iowa	New Mexico	Washington
Kansas	New York	Wisconsin
Louisiana	North Carolina	Wyoming

The Infant Mortality for American Indians and Alaska Natives dropped from 62.7 infant deaths per 1,000 live births in 1954-56 to 9.7 in 1986-1988, a decrease of 85 percent. The US All Races rate for 1987 was 10.1.

The IHS (both IHS & Tribes) operated 50 hospitals and 450 outpatient clinics on September 30, 1990. The average size of the hospitals is 25-49 beds (1990 Chart Series).

Drug and Alcohol Rehabilitation

Drug and alcohol rehabilitation services are operated by tribal groups under funding of PL 99-570 and PL 100-690. Approximately 18% of all Indian deaths are due to alcohol related diseases. This legislation under Part C of the law, sets aside special funds for American Indian/Alaska Native populations. This law mandates comprehensive alcohol/drug program development for both youth and adults. Included are prevention, inpatient, outpatient, aftercare, outreach, community education, tribal action plans and collaboration between the Bureau of Indian Affairs, the Indian Health Service and tribal governments.

Alcoholism Death Rates

In 1988, the age-adjusted alcoholism death rate for American Indians and Alaska Natives was at its highest level since 1981. It was 33.9 deaths per 100,000 population or 5.4 times the US All Races rate of 6.3.

Suicide death rates are closely related to substance abuse rates. The following suicide rates are by age group for 1986-1988 for American Indians and Alaska Natives, Rate per 100,000 population.

Age Group	Both Sexes
5-14 years	1.7
15-24 years	23.6
25-34 years	28.7
35-44 years	19.6
45-54 years	13.1
55-64 years	8.3
65-74 years	9.0
76-85 years	7.5
85 years +	5.3

In response to these tragic statistics Congress passed the Omnibus Drug Bill known as the "Indian Alcohol and Substance Abuse Prevention and Treatment Act of 1986". A copy of the general provisions are as follows:

PART I - General Provisions

SEC. 4202. FINDINGS.

The Congress finds and declares that--

    (1) the Federal Government has a historical relationship and unique legal and moral responsibility to Indian tribes and their members,

    (2) included in this responsibility is the treaty, statutory, and historical obligation to assist the Indian tribes in meeting the health and social needs of their members,

    (3) alcoholism and alcohol and substance abuse is the most severe health and social problem facing Indian tribes and people today and nothing is more costly to Indian people than the consequences of alcohol and substance abuse measured in physical, mental, social, and economic terms,

    (4) alcohol and substance abuse is the leading generic risk factor among Indians, and Indians die from alcoholism at over 4 times the age-adjusted rates for the United States population and alcohol and substance misuse results in a rate of years of potential life lost nearly 5 times that of the United States,

    (5) 4 of the top 10 causes of death among Indians are alcohol and drug related injuries (18 percent of all deaths), chronic liver disease and cirrhosis (5 percent), suicide (3 percent), and homicide (3 percent),

    (6) primarily because deaths from unintentional injuries and violence occur disproportionately among young people, the age-specific death rate for Indians is approximately double the United States rate for the 15 to 45 age group,

    (7) Indians between the ages of 15 and 24 years of age are more than 2 times as likely to commit suicide as the general population and approximately 80 percent of those suicides are alcohol-related,

    (8) Indians between the ages of 15 and 24 years of age are twice as likely as the general population to die in automobile accidents, 75 percent of which are alcohol-related,

    (9) the Indian Health Service, which is charged with treatment and rehabilitation efforts, has directed only 1 percent of its budget for alcohol and substance abuse programs,

    (10) the Bureau of Indian Affairs, which has responsibility for programs in education, social services, law enforcement, and other areas, has assumed little responsibility for coordinating its various efforts to focus on the epidemic of alcohol and substance abuse among Indian people,

    (11) this lack of emphasis and priority continues despite the fact that Bureau of Indian Affairs and Indian Health Service officials publicly acknowledge that alcohol and substance abuse among Indians is the most serious health and social problem facing the Indian people, and

(12) the Indian tribes have the primary responsibility for protecting and ensuring the well-being of their members and the resources made available under this subtitle will assist Indian tribes in meeting that responsibility.

SEC. 4203. PURPOSE.

It is the purpose of this subtitle to--

(1) authorize and develop a comprehensive, coordinated attack upon the illegal narcotics traffic in Indian country and the deleterious impact of alcohol and substance abuse upon Indian tribes and their members,

(2) provide needed direction and guidance to those Federal agencies responsible for Indian programs to identify and focus existing programs and resources, including those made available by this subtitle, upon this problem,

(3) provide authority and opportunities for Indian tribes to develop and implement a coordinated program for the prevention and treatment of alcohol and substance abuse at the local level, and

(4) to modify or supplement existing programs and authorities in the areas of education, family and social services, law enforcement and judicial services, and health services to further the purposes of this subtitle.

SEC. 4204. DEFINITIONS.

For purposes of this subtitle--

(1) The term "agency" means the local administrative entity of the Bureau of Indian Affairs serving one or more Indian tribes within a defined geographic area.

(2) The term "youth" shall have the meaning given it in any particular Tribal Action Plan adopted pursuant to section 4205, except that, for purposes of statistical reporting under this subtitle, it shall mean a person who is 19 years or younger or who is in attendance at a secondary school.

(3) The term "Indian tribe" means any Indian tribe, band, nation, or other organized group or community of Indians (including any Alaska Native village or regional or village corporation as defined in, or established pursuant to, the Alaska Native Claims Settlement Act (43 U.S.C. 1601 et seq.)) which is recognized as eligible for special programs and services provided by the United States to Indians because of their status as Indians.

(4) The term "prevention and treatment" includes, as appropriate--

(A) efforts to identify, and the identification of, Indians who are at risk with respect to, or who are abusers of, alcohol or controlled substances,

(B) intervention into cases of on-going alcohol and substance abuse to halt a further progression of such abuse,

(C) prevention through education and the provision of alternative activities,

(D) treatment for alcohol and substance abusers to help abstain from, and alleviate the effects of, abuse,

(E) rehabilitation to provide on-going assistance, either on an inpatient or outpatient basis, to help Indians reform or abstain from alcohol or substance abuse,

(F) follow-up or after-care to provide the appropriate counseling and assistance on an outpatient basis, and

(G) referral to other sources of assistance or resources.

(5) The term "service unit" means an administrative entity within the Indian Health Service or a tribe or tribal organization operating health care programs or facilities with funds from the Indian Health Service under the Indian Self-Determination Act through which the services are provided, directly or by contract, to the eligible Indian population within a defined geographic area.

PART II - Coordination of Resources and Programs

SEC. 4205. Inter-Departmental Memorandum of Agreement

(a) IN GENERAL--Not later than 120 days after the date of enactment of this subtitle, the Secretary of the Interior and the Secretary of Health and Human Services shall develop and enter into a Memorandum of Agreement which shall, among other things--

(1) determine and define the scope of the problem of alcohol and substance abuse for Indian tribes and their members and its financial and human costs, and specifically identify such problems affecting Indian youth,

(2) identify--

(A) the resources and programs of the Bureau of Indian Affairs and Indian Health Service, and

(B) other Federal, tribal, State and local, and private resources and programs, which would be relevant to a coordinated effort to combat alcohol and substance abuse among Indian people, including those programs and resources made available by this subtitle,

(3) develop and establish appropriate minimum standards for each agency's program responsibilities under the Memorandum of Agreement which may be--

(A) the existing Federal or State standards in effect, or

(B) in the absence of such standards, new standards which will be developed and established in consultation with Indian tribes,

(4) coordinate the Bureau of Indian Affairs and Indian Health Service alcohol and substance abuse programs existing on the date of the enactment of this subtitle with programs or efforts established by this subtitle,

(5) delineate the responsibilities of the Bureau of Indian Affairs and the Indian Health Service to coordinate alcohol and substance abuse-related services at the central, area, agency, and service unit levels,

(6) direct Bureau of Indian Affairs agency and education superintendents, where appropriate, and the Indian Health Service service unit directors to cooperate fully with tribal requests made pursuant to section 4206, and

(7) provide for an annual review of such agreements by the Secretary of the Interior and the Secretary of Health and Human Services.

(b) CHARACTER OF ACTIVITIES.--To the extent that there are new activities undertaken pursuant to this subtitle, those activities shall supplement, not supplant, activities, programs, and local actions that are ongoing on the date of the enactment of this subtitle. Such activities shall be undertaken in the manner least disruptive to tribal control, in accordance with the Indian Self-Determination and Education Assistance Act (25 U.S.C. 450 et seq.), and local control, in accordance with section 1130 of the Education Amendments of 1978 (25 U.S.C. 2010).

(c) CONSULTATION.--The Secretary of the Interior and the Secretary of Health and Human Services shall, in developing the Memorandum of Agreement under subsection (a), consult with and solicit the comments of--

(1) interested Indian tribes,

(2) Indian individuals,

(3) Indian organizations, and

(4) professionals in the treatment of alcohol and substance abuse.

(d) PUBLICATION.--The Memorandum of Agreement under subsection (a) shall be submitted to Congress and published in the Federal Register not later than 130 days after the date of enactment of this subtitle. At the same time as publication in the Federal Register, the Secretary of the Interior shall provide a copy of this subtitle and the Memorandum of Agreement under subsection (a) to each Indian tribe.

SEC. 4206. TRIBAL ACTION PLANS.

(a) IN GENERAL.--The governing body of any Indian tribe may, at its discretion, adopt a resolution for the establishment of a Tribal Action Plan to coordinate available resources and programs, including programs and resources made available by this subtitle, in an effort to combat alcohol and substance abuse among its members. Such resolution shall be the basis for the implementation of this subtitle and of the Memorandum of Agreement under section 4205.

(b) COOPERATION.--At the request of any Indian tribe pursuant to a resolution adopted under subsection (a), the Bureau of Indian Affair agency and education superintendents, where appropriate, and the Indian Health Service unit director providing services to such tribe shall cooperate with the tribe in the development of a Tribal Action Plan to coordinate resources and programs relevant to alcohol and substance abuse prevention and treatment. Upon the development of such a plan, such superintendents and director, as directed by the Memorandum of Agreement established under section 4205, shall enter into an agreement with the tribe for the implementation of the Tribal Action Plan under subsection (a).

(c) PROVISIONS.--

(1) Any Tribal Action Plan entered into under subsection (b) shall provide for--

(A) the establishment of a Tribal Coordinating Committee which shall--

(i) at a minimum, have as members a tribal representative who shall serve as Chairman and the Bureau of Indian Affairs agency and education superintendents, where appropriate, and the Indian Health Service service unit director, or their representatives,

(ii) have primary responsibility for the implementation of the Tribal Action Plan,

(iii) have the responsibility for on-going review and evaluation of, and the making of recommendations to the tribe relating to, the Tribal Action Plan, and

(iv) have the responsibility for scheduling Federal, tribal or other personnel for training in the prevention and treatment of alcohol and substance abuse among Indians as provided under section 4228, and

(B) the incorporation of the minimum standards for those programs and services which it encompasses which shall be--

(i) the Federal or State standards as provided in section 4205(a)(3), or

(2) Any Tribal Action Plan may, among other things, provide for--

(A) an assessment of the scope of the problem of alcohol and substance abuse for the Indian tribe which adopted the resolution for the Plan.

(B) the identification and coordination of available resources and programs relevant to a program of alcohol and substance abuse prevention and treatment,

(C) the establishment and prioritization of goals and the efforts needed to meet those goals, and

(D) the identification of community and family roles in any of the efforts undertaken as part of the Tribal Action Plan.

(d) GRANTS.--

(1) The Secretary of the Interior may make grants to Indian tribes adopting a resolution pursuant to subsection (a) to provide technical assistance in the development of a Tribal Action Plan. The Secretary shall allocate funds based on need.

(2) There is authorized to be appropriated not to exceed $1,000,000 for each of the fiscal year 1987, 1988, and 1989 for grants under this subsection.

(e) FEDERAL ACTION.--If any Indian tribe does not adopt a resolution as provided in subsection (a) within 90 days after the publication of the Memorandum of Agreement in the Federal Register as provided in section 4205, the Secretary of the Interior and the Secretary of Health and Human Services shall require the Bureau of Indian Affairs agency and education superintendents, where appropriate, and the Indian Health Service unit director serving such tribe to enter into an agreement to identify and coordinate available programs and resources to carry out the purposes of this subtitle for such tribe. After such an agreement has been entered into for a tribe such tribe may adopt a resolution under subsection (a).

SEC. 4207. DEPARTMENTAL RESPONSIBILITY

(a) IMPLEMENTATION.--The Secretary of the Interior, acting through the Bureau of Indian Affairs, and the Secretary of Health and Human Services, acting through the Indian Health Service, shall bear equal responsibility for the implementation of this subtitle in cooperation with Indian tribes.

(b) OFFICE OF ALCOHOL AND SUBSTANCE ABUSE.--

(1) In order to better coordinate the various programs of the Bureau of Indian Affairs in carrying out this subtitle, there is established within the Office of the Assistant Secretary of Indian Affairs an Office of Alcohol and Substance Abuse. The director of such office shall be appointed by the Assistant Secretary on a permanent basis at no less than a grade GS-15 of the General Schedule.

(2) In addition to other responsibilities which may be assigned to such Office, it shall be responsible for--

(A) monitoring the performance and compliance of programs of the Bureau of Indian Affairs in meeting the goals and purposes of this subtitle and the Memorandum of Agreement entered into under section 4205, and

(B) serving as a point of contact within the Bureau of Indian Affairs for Indian tribes and the Tribal Coordinating Committees regarding the implementation of this subtitle, the Memorandum of Agreement, and any Tribal Action Plan established under section 4206.

(c) INDIAN YOUTH PROGRAMS OFFICER.--

(1) There is established in the Office of Alcohol and Substance Abuse the position to be known as the Indian Youth Programs Officer.

(2) The position of Indian Youth Programs Officer shall be established on a permanent basis at no less than the grade of GS-14 of the General Schedule.

(3) In addition to other responsibilities which may be assigned to the Indian Youth Programs Officer relating to Indian Youth, such Officer shall be responsible for--

(A) monitoring the performance and compliance of programs of the Bureau of Indian Affairs in meeting the goals and purposes of this subtitle and the Memorandum of Agreement entered into under section 4205 as they relate to Indian youth efforts, and

(B) providing advice and recommendations, including recommendations submitted by Indian tribes and Tribal Coordinating Committees, to the Director of the Office of Alcohol and Substance Abuse as they relate to Indian youth.

SEC. 4208. CONGRESSIONAL INTENT.

It is the intent of Congress that--

(1) specific Federal laws, and administrative regulations promulgated thereunder, establishing programs of the Bureau of Indian Affairs, the Indian Health Service, and other Federal agencies, and

(2) general Federal laws, including laws limiting augmentation of Federal appropriations or encouraging joint or cooperative funding,

shall be liberally construed and administered to achieve the purposes of this subtitle.

SEC. 4209. FEDERAL FACILITIES, PROPERTY, AND EQUIPMENT.

(a) FACILITY AVAILABILITY.--In the furtherance of the purposes and goals of this subtitle, the Secretary of the Interior, and the Secretary of Health and Human Services shall make available for community use, to the extent permitted by law and as may be provided in a Tribal Action Plan, local Federal facilities, property, and equipment, including school facilities. Such facility availability shall include school facilities under the Secretary of the Interior jurisdiction: Provided, That the use of any school facilities shall be conditioned upon approval of the local school board with jurisdiction over such school.

(b) COSTS.--Any additional cost associated with the use of Federal facilities, property, or equipment under subsection (a) may be born by the Secretary of the Interior and the Secretary of Health and Human Services out of available Federal, tribal, State, local, or private funds, if not otherwise prohibited by law. This subsection does not require the Secretary of the Interior nor the Secretary of Health and Human Services to expend additional funds to meet the additional costs which may be associated with the provision of such facilities, property or equipment for community use. Where the use of Federal facilities, property, or equipment under subsection (a) furthers the purposes and goals of this subtitle, the use of funds other than those funds appropriated to the Department of the Interior or the Department of Health and Human Services to meet the additional costs associated with such use shall not constitute an augmentation of Federal appropriations.

SEC. 4210. NEWSLETTER.

The Secretary of the Interior shall, not later than 120 days after the date of the enactment of this subtitle, publish an alcohol and substance abuse newsletter in cooperation with the Secretary of Health and Human Services and the Secretary of Education to report on Indian alcohol and substance abuse projects and programs. The newsletter shall--

(1) be published once in each calendar quarter,

(2) include reviews of programs determined by the Secretary of the Interior to be exemplary and provide sufficient information to enable interested persons to obtain further information about such programs, and

(3) be circulated without charge to--

(A) schools,

(B) tribal offices,

(C) Bureau of Indian Affairs' agency and area offices,

(D) Indian Health Service area and service unit offices,

(E) Indian Health Service alcohol programs, and

(F) other entities providing alcohol and substance abuse related services or resources to Indian people.

PART III - Indian Youth Programs

SEC. 4211. REVIEW OF PROGRAMS.

(a) REVIEW.--In the development of the Memorandum of Agreement required by section 4205, the Secretary of the Interior and the Secretary of Health and Human Services, in cooperation with the Secretary of Education shall review and consider--

(1) Federal programs providing education services resources or benefits to Indian children,

(2) tribal, State, local, and private educational resources and programs,

(3) Federal programs providing family and social services and benefits for Indian families and children,

(4) Federal programs relating to youth employment, recreation, cultural, and community activities, and

(5) tribal, State, local, and private resources for programs similar to those cited in paragraphs (3) and (4),

to determine their applicability and relevance in carrying out the purposes of this subtitle.

(b) PUBLICATION.--The results of the review conducted under subsection (a) shall be provided to each Indian tribe as soon as possible for their consideration and use in the development or modification of a Tribal Action Plan under section 4206.

SEC. 4212. INDIAN EDUCATION PROGRAMS.

(a) PILOT PROGRAMS.--The Assistant Secretary of Indian Affairs shall develop and implement pilot programs in selected schools funded by the Bureau of Indian Affairs (subject to the approval of the local school board or contract school board) to determine the effectiveness of summer youth programs in furthering the purposes and goals of the Indian Alcohol and Substance Abuse Prevention Act of 1986. The Assistant Secretary shall defray all costs associated with the actual operation and support of the pilot programs in the school from funds appropriated for this section. For the pilot programs there are authorized to be appropriated such sums as may be necessary for each of the fiscal years 1987, 1988, and 1989.

(b) USE OF FUNDS.--Federal financial assistance made available to public or private schools because of the enrollment of Indian children pursuant to--

(1) the Act of April 16, 1934, as amended by the Indian Education Assistance Act (25 U.S.C. 452 et seq.),

(2) the Indian Elementary and Secondary School Assistance Act (20 U.S.C. 241aa et seq.), and

(3) the Indian Education Act (20 U.S.C. 3885),

may be used to support a program of instruction relating to alcohol and substance abuse prevention and treatment.

SEC. 4213. EMERGENCY SHELTERS.

(a) IN GENERAL.--A Tribal Action Plan adopted pursuant to section 4206 may make such provisions as may be necessary and practical for the establishment, funding, licensing, and operation of emergency shelters or half-way houses for Indian youth who have been arrested for offenses directly or indirectly related to alcohol or substance abuse.

(b) REFERRALS.--

(1) In any case where an Indian youth is arrested or detained by the Bureau of Indian Affairs or tribal law enforcement personnel for an offense relating to alcohol or substance abuse, other than for a status offense as defined by the

Juvenile Justice and Delinquency Prevention Act of 1974, under circumstances where such youth may not be immediately restored to the custody of his parents or guardians and where there is space available in an appropriately licensed and supervised emergency shelter or half-way house, such youth shall be referred to such facility in lieu of incarceration in a secured facility unless such youth is deemed a danger to himself or to other persons.

(2) In any case where there is a space available in an appropriately licensed and supervised emergency shelter or half-way house, the Bureau of Indian Affairs and tribal courts are encouraged to refer Indian youth convicted of offenses directly or indirectly related to alcohol and substance abuse to such facilities in lieu of sentencing to incarceration in a secured juvenile facility.

(c) DIRECTION TO STATES.--In the case of any State that exercises criminal jurisdiction over any part of Indian country under section 1162 of title 18 of the United States Code or section 401 of the Act of April 11, 1968 (25 U.S.C. 1321), such State is urged to require its law enforcement officers to--

(1) place any Indian youth arrested for any offense related to alcohol or substance abuse in a temporary emergency shelter described in subsection (d) or a community-based alcohol or substance abuse treatment facility in lieu of incarceration to the extent such facilities are available, and

(2) observe the standards promulgated under subsection (d).

(d) STANDARDS.--The Assistant Secretary of Indian Affairs shall, as part of the development of the Memorandum of Agreement set out in section 4205, promulgate standards by which the emergency shelters established under a program pursuant to subsection (a) shall be established and operated.

(e) AUTHORIZATION.--For the planning and design, construction, and renovation of emergency shelters or half-way houses to provide emergency care for Indian youth, there is authorized to be appropriated $3,000,000 for each of the fiscal years 1987, 1988, and 1989. The Secretary of the Interior shall allocate funds appropriated pursuant to this subsection on the basis of priority of need of the various Indian tribes and such funds, when allocated, shall be subject to contracting pursuant to the Indian Self-Determination Act.

SEC. 4214. SOCIAL SERVICES REPORTS.

(a) DATA.--The Secretary of the Interior, with respect to the administration of any family or social services program by the Bureau of Indian Affairs directly or through contracts under the Indian Self-Determination Act, shall require the compilation of data relating to the number and types of child abuse and neglect cases seen and the type of assistance provided. Additionally, such data should also be categorized to reflect those cases that involve, or appear to involve, alcohol and substance abuse, those cases which are recurring, and those cases which involve other minor siblings.

(b) REFERRAL OF DATA.--The data compiled pursuant to subsection (a) shall be provided annually to the affected Indian tribe and Tribal Coordinating Committee to assist them in developing or modifying a Tribal Action Plan and shall also be submitted to the Indian Health Service service unit director who will have responsibility for compiling a tribal comprehensive report as provided in section 4230.

(c) CONFIDENTIALITY.--In carrying out the requirements of subsections (a) and (b), the Secretary shall insure that the data is compiled and reported in a manner which will preserve the confidentiality of the families and individuals.

PART IV - Law Enforcement and Judicial Services

SEC. 4215. REVIEW OF PROGRAMS.

(a) LAW ENFORCEMENT AND JUDICIAL SERVICES.--In the development of the Memorandum of Agreement required by section 4205, the Secretary of the Interior and the Secretary of Health and Human Services, in cooperation with the Attorney General of the United States, shall review and consider--

(1) the various programs established by Federal law providing law enforcement or judicial services for Indian tribes, and

(2) tribal and State and local law enforcement and judicial programs and systems,

to determine their applicability and relevance in carrying out the purposes of this subtitle.

(b) DISSEMINATION OF REVIEW.--The results of the review conducted pursuant to subsection (a) shall be made available to every Indian tribe as soon as possible for their consideration and use in the development and modification of a Tribal Action Plan.

SEC. 4216. ILLEGAL NARCOTICS TRAFFIC ON THE PAPAGO RESERVATION: SOURCE ERADICATION

(aX1) INVESTIGATION AND CONTROL.--The Secretary of the Interior shall provide assistance to the Papago Indian Tribe (Tohono O'odham) of Arizona for the investigation and control of illegal narcotics traffic on the Papago Reservation along the border with Mexico. The Secretary shall ensure that tribal efforts are coordinated with appropriate Federal law enforcement agencies, including the United States Customs Service.

(2) AUTHORIZATIONS.--For the purpose of providing the assistance required by subsection (a), there is authorized to be appropriated $500,000 for each of the fiscal years 1987, 1989, and 1989.

(bX1) MARIJUANA ERADICATION.--The Secretary of the Interior, in cooperation with appropriated Federal, tribal, and State and local law enforcement agencies, shall establish and implement a program for the eradication of marijuana cultivation within Indian country as defined in section 1152 of title 18, United States Code. The Secretary shall establish a priority for the use of funds appropriated under subsection (b) for those Indian reservations where the scope of the problem is most critical, and such funds shall be available for contracting by Indian tribes pursuant to the Indian Self-Determination Act.

(2) AUTHORIZATIONS.--To carry out subsection (a), there is authorized to be appropriated such sums as may be necessary for each of the fiscal years 1987, 1988, and 1989.

PART V - Bureau of Indian Affairs Law Enforcement

SEC. 4217. TRIBAL COURTS, SENTENCING AND FINES.

To enhance the ability of tribal governments to prevent and penalize the traffic of illegal narcotics on Indian reservations, paragraph (7) of section 202 of the Act of April 11, 1969 (25 U.S.C. 1302) is amended by striking out "for a term of six months and a fine of $500, or both" and inserting in lieu thereof "for a term of one year and a fine of $5,000, or both".

SEC. 4218. BUREAU OF INDIAN AFFAIRS LAW ENFORCEMENT AND JUDICIAL TRAINING

(a) IN GENERAL.--The Secretary of the Interior shall ensure, through the establishment of a new training program or through the supplement of existing training programs, that all Bureau of Indian Affairs and tribal law enforcement and judicial personnel shall have available training in the investigation and prosecution of offenses relating to illegal narcotics and in alcohol substance abuse prevention and treatment. Any training provided to Bureau of Indian Affairs and tribal law enforcement and judicial personnel as provided in subsection (a) shall specifically include training in the problems of youth alcohol and substance abuse prevention and treatment. Such training shall be coordinated with the Indian Health Service in the carrying out of its responsibilities under section 4228.

SEC. 4219. MEDICAL ASSESSMENT AND TREATMENT OF JUVENILE OFFENDERS.

The Memorandum of Agreement entered into pursuant to section 4205 shall include a specific provision for the development and implementation at each Bureau of Indian Affair agency and Indian Health Service unit of a procedure for the emergency medical assessment and treatment of every Indian youth arrested or detained by Bureau of Indian

Affairs or tribal law enforcement personnel for an offense relating to or involving alcohol or substance abuse. The medical assessment required by this subsection--

(1) shall be conducted to determine the mental or physical state of the individual assessed so that appropriate steps can be taken to protect the individual's health and well-being,

(2) shall occur as soon as possible after the arrest or detention of an Indian youth, and

(3) shall be provided by the Indian Health Service, either through its direct or contract health service.

SEC. 4220. JUVENILE DETENTION CENTERS.

(a) PLAN.--The Secretary of the Interior shall construct or renovate and staff new or existing juvenile detention centers. The Secretary shall ensure that the construction and operation of the centers is consistent with the Juvenile Justice and Delinquency Prevention Act of 1974.

(b) AUTHORIZATION.--For the purpose of subsection (a), there is authorized to be appropriated $10,000,000 for construction and renovation for each of the fiscal years 1987, 1988, and 1989, and $5,000,000 for staffing and operation of each of the fiscal years 1987, 1988, and 1989.

SEC. 4221. MODEL INDIAN JUVENILE CODE.

The Secretary of the Interior, either directly or by contract, shall provide for the development of a Model Indian Juvenile Code which shall be consistent with the Juvenile Justice and Delinquency Prevention Act of 1974 and which shall include provisions relating to the disposition of cases involving Indian youth arrested or detained by Bureau of Indian Affairs or tribal law enforcement personnel for alcohol or drug related offenses. The development of such model code shall be accomplished in cooperation with Indian organizations having an expertise or knowledge in the field of law enforcement and judicial procedure and in consultation with Indian tribes. Upon completion of the Model Code, the Secretary shall make copies available to each Indian tribe.

SEC. 4222. LAW ENFORCEMENT AND JUDICIAL REPORT.

(a) COMPILATION OF LAW ENFORCEMENT DATA.--The Secretary of the Interior, with respect to the administration of any law enforcement or judicial services program by the Bureau of Indian Affairs, either directly or through contracts under the Indian Self-Determination Act, shall require the compilation of data relating to calls and encounters, arrests and detentions, and disposition of cases by Bureau of Indian Affairs or tribal law enforcement or judicial personnel involving Indians where it is determined that alcohol or substance abuse is a contribution factor.

(b) REFERRAL OF DATA.--The data compiled pursuant to subsection (a) shall be provided annually to the affected Indian tribe and Tribal Coordinating Committee to assist them in developing or modifying a Tribal Action Plan and shall also be submitted to the Indian Health Service unit director who will have the responsibility for compiling a tribal comprehensive report as provided in section 4230.

(c) CONFIDENTIALITY.--In carrying out this section, the Secretary shall insure that the data is compiled and reported in a manner which will preserve the confidentiality of families and individuals involved.

PART VI - Indian Alcohol and Substance Abuse
Treatment and Rehabilitation

SEC. 4224. REVIEW OF PROGRAMS.

(a) IN GENERAL.--In the development of the Memorandum of Agreement required by section 4205, the Secretary of the Interior and the Secretary of Health and Human Services shall review and consider--

(1) the various programs established by Federal law providing health services and benefits to Indian tribes, including those relating to mental health and alcohol and substance abuse prevention and treatment,

(2) tribal, State and local, and private health resources and programs,

(3) where facilities to provide such treatment are or should be located, and

(4) the effectiveness of public and private alcohol and substance abuse treatment programs in operation on the date of the enactment of this subtitle, to determine their applicability and relevance in carrying out the purposes of this subtitle.

(b) DISSEMINATION.--The results of the review conducted under subsection (a) shall be provided to every Indian tribe as soon as possible for their consideration and use in the development or modification of a Tribal Action Plan.

SEC. 4225. INDIAN HEALTH SERVICE RESPONSIBILITIES.

The Memorandum of Agreement entered into pursuant to section 4205 shall include specific provisions pursuant to which the Indian Health Service shall assume responsibility for--

(1) the determination of the scope of the problem of alcohol and substance abuse among Indian people, including the number of Indians within the jurisdiction of the Indian Health Service who are directly or indirectly affected by alcohol and substance abuse and the financial and human cost.

    (2) an assessment of the existing and needed resources necessary for the prevention of alcohol and substance abuse and the treatment of Indians affected by alcohol and substance abuse, and

    (3) an estimate of the funding necessary to adequately support a program of prevention of alcohol and substance abuse and treatment of Indians affected by alcohol and substance abuse.

SEC. 4226. INDIAN HEALTH SERVICE PROGRAMS.

The Secretary of Health and Human Services, acting through the Indian Health Service, shall provide a program of comprehensive alcohol and substance abuse prevention and treatment which shall include--

    (1) prevention, through educational intervention, in Indian communities,

    (2) acute detoxification and treatment,

    (3) community-based rehabilitation, and

    (4) community education and involvement, including extensive training of health care, educational, and community-based personnel.

The target population of such a program shall be the members of Indian tribes. Additionally, efforts to train and educate key members of the Indian community shall target employees of health, education, judicial, law enforcement, legal, and social service programs.

SEC. 4227. INDIAN HEALTH SERVICE YOUTH PROGRAM

    (a) DETOXIFICATION AND REHABILITATION.--The Secretary shall develop and implement a program for acute detoxification and treatment for Indian youth who are alcohol and substance abusers. The program shall include regional treatment centers designed to include detoxification and rehabilitation for both sexes on a referral basis. These regional centers shall be integrated with the intake and rehabilitation programs based in the referring Indian community.

    (b) CENTERS.--The Secretary shall construct or renovate a youth regional treatment center in each area under the jurisdiction of an Indian Health Service area office. For purposes of the preceding sentence, the area offices of the Indian Health Service in Tucson and Phoenix, Arizona, shall be considered one area office. The regional treatment centers shall be appropriately staffed with health professionals. There are authorized to be appropriated $6,000,000 for the construction and renovation of the regional youth treatment centers, and $3,000,000 for the staffing of such centers, for each of the fiscal years 1987, 1988, and 1989.

    (c) FEDERALLY OWNED STRUCTURES.--

    (1) The Secretary of Health and Human Services, acting through the Indian

Health Service, shall, in consultation with Indian tribes--

    (A) identify and use, where appropriate, federally owned structures, suitable as local residential or regional alcohol and substance abuse treatment centers for Indian youth, and

    (B) establish guidelines for determining the suitability of any such federally owned structure to be used as a local residential or regional alcohol and substance abuse treatment center for Indian youth.

    (2) Any structure described in paragraph (1) may be used under such terms and conditions as may be agreed upon by the Secretary of Health and Human Services and the agency having responsibility for the structure.

    (3) There are authorized to be appropriated $3,000,000 for each of the fiscal years 1987, 1988, and 1989.

(d) REHABILITATION AND FOLLOW-UP SERVICES.--

    (1) The Secretary, in cooperation with the Secretary of the Interior, shall develop and implement within each Indian Health Service service unit community-based rehabilitation and follow-up services for Indian youth who are alcohol or substance abusers which are designed to integrate long-term treatment and to monitor and support the Indian youth after their return to their home community.

    (2) Services under paragraph (1) shall be administered within each service unit by trained staff within the community who can assist the Indian youth in continuing development of self-image, positive problem-solving skills, and nonalcohol or substance abusing behaviors. Such staff shall include alcohol and substance abuse counselors, mental health professionals, and other health professionals and paraprofessionals, including community health representatives.

    (3) For the purpose of providing the services authorized by paragraph (1), there are authorized to be appropriated $9,000,000 for each of the fiscal years 1987, 1988, and 1989.

SEC. 1228. TRAINING AND COMMUNITY EDUCATION.

    (a) COMMUNITY EDUCATION.--The Secretary, in cooperation with the Secretary of the Interior, shall develop and implement within each service unit a program of community education and involvement which shall be designed to provide concise and timely information to the community leadership of each tribal community. Such program shall include education in alcohol and substance abuse to the critical core of each tribal community, including political leaders, tribal judges, law enforcement personnel, members of tribal health and education boards, and other critical parties.

    (b) TRAINING.--The Secretary of Health and Human Services shall, either directly or through contract, provide instruction in the area of alcohol and substance abuse, including instruction in crisis intervention and family relations in the context of alcohol and substance abuse, youth alcohol and substance abuse, and the causes and effects of fetal alcohol syndrome to appropriate employees of the Bureau of Indian Affairs and the Indian Health Service, and personnel in schools or programs operated under any contract with the Bureau of Indian Affairs or the Indian Health Service, including supervisors of emergency shelters and half-way houses described in section 4213.

(cX1) DEMONSTRATION PROGRAM.--The Secretary of Health and Human Services shall establish at least one demonstration project to determine the most effective and cost-efficient means of--

(A) providing health promotion and disease prevention services.

(B) encouraging Indians to adopt good health habits.

(C) reducing health risks to Indians, particularly the risks of heart disease, cancer, stroke, diabetes, depression, and lifestyle-related accidents.

Alcohol Programs Funded by the Indian Health Service

Thanks to the tribal efforts to address alcoholism/substance abuse, Congress has appropriated more than 50 million dollars annually to fight this problem among Indian tribes. Because it is difficult to measure educational/prevention efforts in impacting this problem steps are being taken to improve the success rates of intervention.

One cannot separate substance abuse in Indian communities from the poverty, unemployment, racism, high school dropout and boredom that exists among the Indian population. To exist as a conquered people with the constant erosion of sovereignty in every area of tribal life, resistance to assimilation and strong cultural and spiritual beliefs, the challenges to American Indians/Alaska Natives are endless. To look at substance abuse in a vacuum feeds into institutional racism and continued oppression of tribal populations. Though a clinical approach is important, it must be a part of a comprehensive holistic model of empowerment of Indian communities. This model must include economic development, validation of traditional spiritual practices of Indian tribes, community education and prevention and additional options to the 12 step model of recovery. Though Gaming establishments have been criticized by some of the Indian leaders, they have created jobs and revenue to fund social services, health services and education for tribal members.

Community Organization and Empowerment

Because alcohol and other drug abuse is related to suicides, spousal abuse, traffic fatalities, assaults, murders, drownings, child abuse, rape and HIV infection it is a major threat to tribal communities. Community organization and empowerments are important parts of the Holistic approach. The following factors are important in addressing this issue

1. Prevention is holistic, mind, body and spirit are interrelated.
2. Alcohol/substance abuse is a symptom of larger problems (i.e., acculturated stress).
3. The individual is an extension of the community.
4. Incorporate indigenous practices and values.
5. Involve the community in planning, research and ownership.
6. Recognize and understand the culture of the community.
7. Research must identify biological, psycho-social risk factors in the community.
8. Living life consistently with relationships as designed, take back control of life.
9. Achieve balance with indigenous concepts of order/life.
10. Focus on positive elements.
11. Integrate indigenous/traditional healing methods into Technical Assistance, and clinical services.
12. Include elders in the promotion of traditional culture.
13. Encourage and insure use of language in services.
14. Encourage activities that promote native practices.
15. Educate service providers/policy and others.
16. In promotion of research, allow communities to define research goals.
17. Develop protocol researchers must observe to get into the community.
18. Use authorized "Local" talent before someone else is considered (AMAP i.e., indigenous peoples). (NIAAA Special report to Congress, 1987).

Successes in Interventions with Tribal Groups

Several model programs should be mentioned as having a major impact in the area of prevention. First mentioned is the Alkali tribal community in Canada. This community has successfully decreased the rate of addiction and abuse from 90% to less than 5% of the population in a period of 10 years by using a community development model which included clinical services. A film portraying the steps in achieving this goal was produced, titled THE HONOR OF ONE IS THE HONOR OF ALL. Celia Fire Thunder, a Lakota nurse has been successful in organizing communities among the Sioux/Lakota tribe in South Dakota in the areas of domestic violence/substance abuse and other problems associated with alcohol and drug abuse. Several tribes in California have voted to require total drug and alcohol abstinence of Health Board members as a requirement for serving on the boards; other tribes require total abstinence of clinical staff employed by Health Clinics in California. Many other model prevention programs are being implemented throughout Indian country which incorporate healthy lifestyles and physical exercise and diet as important factors in intervention programs.

3. AMERICAN INDIAN VALUES

The Concept of Values and the Historical Development

A growing body of literature postulates that there is a core of common values within each population despite the recognized diversity of subgroups. although there are degrees of cultural diversity among the subgroups, e.g. those between English and Italian ancestry in the Anglo-American population, the tribal diversity among the American Indian population, these diversities are overshadowed by the degree of homogeneity found within each of the ethnic populations.

The President's Commission on Mental Health Report (1979, p.19) states:

Mental health of American Indians and Alaska Natives cannot be viewed in the context of traditional Western mental health world which has no understanding of the Indian world and the unique characteristics and personality structures of aboriginal peoples. Any discussion or definition of mental health as it relates to Indian peoples must take place in the context of Indian peoples' history and in their strengths and culture. This includes all Indian peoples no matter what their setting.

Values are significant since they permeate the lifestyle of the individual and his world. It is important for educators and other human service personnel to be aware of the different value orientations of American Indians and other ethnic groups since life experiences are defined according to individual values.

Kluckhohn's Theory of value orientation has been selected as the most comprehensive and appropriate model since it has been tested with consistent results over a period of twenty years. Theoretical predictions, made on the basis of anthropological data collected over a period of seven years, were corroborated by the data. In only a very

From "American Indian Values: Critical Factor in Casework" by W. DuBray, Social Casework (January 1985), Vol. 66, No. 1, pp. 30-37, Copyright 1985, Family Service America. Reprinted by permission.

few instances was there a marked discrepancy between the prediction ventured and the result observed. No two cultures surveyed chose exactly the same patterns of preference on any of the orientations. In addition, the degree of similarity and difference proved to be, on the whole, the expected one.

An instrument called the Value Schedule was devised in support of this theory. The Value Schedule, by means of the wording of the situations presented, measured value orientations reflecting patterns of family organization, economic activity, intellectual interest, religious belief and ritual, political behavior, attitudes toward education and numerous other interests.

This instrument was devised in support of this theory and tested cross-culturally with two Anglo-American groups, one Spanish-American group, and two American Indian tribal groups.

First, the theory assumes that there is a limited number of common human problems for which all people at all times must find some solution. A second assumption is that, while there is variability in the solutions of all problems, these are neither limitless nor random but are within a definite range of possible solutions. The third assumption, the one which provides the main key to the analysis of value orientation, is that all alternatives of all solutions are present in all societies at all times, but are differentially preferred. Every society has a dominant profile of value orientation.

Four problems have been singled out as the crucial ones common to all human groups. After the questions are the titles of categories of value orientation:
1.   What is the modality of human activity? (activity orientation)
2.   What is the modality of man's relationship to others? (relational orientation)
3.   What is the temporary focus of human life? (time orientation)
4.   What is the relationship of man to nature? (man/nature orientation)

Philosophers over the years have based differences in activity orientation upon distinctions between Being and Doing. The activity orientation centers on man's mode of self-expression in activity.   The Being orientation gives preference for spontaneous expression of what is inherently "given" in the human personality.   It is a nondevelopmental conception of activity. The Doing orientation demands activity which results in accomplishments that are measurable by standards external to the individual.

The relational orientation refers to man's relationship to others. It has three subdivisions; the Lineal, the Collateral and the Individualistic. If the Lineal principle is dominant, the most important group goals are the continuity of the group through time and ordered positional succession. A dominant Collateral orientation calls for a primacy of the goals and welfare of laterally extended groups. When the Individualistic principle is dominant, individual goals have primacy over the goals of specific collateral or lineal groups.

Every society must deal with time problems; all have their conceptions of the past, the present and the future. Future-oriented cultures would stress the importance of planning and saving. Present-oriented peoples stress the importance of the here and now. Past-oriented peoples would cling to the traditional manner in which things were done historically.

The man-nature orientation is well known from the works of historians and philosophers. Those who believe that there is little or nothing that can be done to protect themselves from storms or acts of nature considered Subjugated to Nature. The concepts of Harmony with Nature indicates no real separation of man, nature and supernature. Each is an extension of the other and the concept of wholeness derives from their unity. Mastery over Nature is the belief that natural forces are to be overcome. Here, there is an emphasis on technology, e.g. rivers are to be spanned with bridges. Definitions of these possible solutions are presented in Table 1.

TABLE I
Definitions of Possible Solutions to Four Life Problems Identified by Kluckhohn & Strodtbeck

Problem	Solution	Definition
1. Man-nature	1. Subjugation to Nature	little or nothing can be done about the future; simply accept the inevitable
	2. Harmony with Nature	no real separation of man, nature, and supernature; one is simply an extension of the other, a concept of wholeness derives from their unity
	3. Mastery over Nature	natural forces of all kinds are to be overcome and put to use of human beings
2. Time	1. Present	pay little attention to what has happened in the past and regard the future as both vague and unpredictable
	2. Past	nothing new ever happened in the present or would happen in the future; it has all happened before in the far distant past
	3. Future	emphasis is placed on the future; it will be bigger and better; considers the past to be old fashioned and is not content with the present

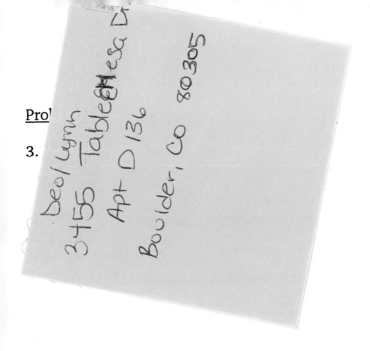

Pro[...]		Definition
3.		preference is for kind of activity which is a spontaneous expression of what is conceived to be "given" in the human personality; non-developmental conception
		demand for kind of activity which results in accomplishments measurable by standards conceived to be external to the acting individual
4. Relational	1. Individualistic	individual goals have primacy over the goals of collateral or lineal groups
	2. Collateral	primacy of goals and welfare of the laterally extended groups
	3. Lineal	group goals have primacy; one of the most important goals is continuity through time

Definition of Values

The earliest value studies of American Indian populations were conducted by social anthropologists. Some anthropologists saw the variation in values of a culture as an interlocking network of dominant, most preferred value orientations and variant value orientations which were both required and permitted (Kluckhohn, 1961).

Although anthropologists have done a great deal to point out value differences between cultures, the process of understanding values has typically employed a psychological level of analysis. Scheibe (1970) defined values as "...what is wanted, was is best, what is preferable, what ought to be done. They suggest the operation of wishes, desires, goals, passions and morals" (P. 42). English and English (1958) indicated that values define for an individual or for a social unit what ends or means to an end are desirable. Both refer to a very generalized set of goal-oriented expectations that are based on a specific process inherent within the person's immediate frame of reference.

Albert (1963) separated values from the actualities of conduct in her definition of values:

> Values are by definition criteria, that is, ideals, goals, norms and standards. Accessible principally through analysis of verbal behavior, values are not the same as the actualities of conduct. Actualization may reveal that values in the fact are not se elegant as they seemed when they were theoretic, shining ideals; that performance does not measure up to intentions; that practice does not vindicate theory. (p. 20) Samler (1966) states that "values are at the heart of the counseling relationship, are reflected in its content and affect the process" (p. 196).

The role of values in counseling is of utmost importance in understanding the client's problem (Ryan, 1976). Much confusion and misunderstanding could be avoided if the counselor takes the time to become acquainted with the values of the client (Trimble, 1976). An example of a values approach to understanding people is that of Vogt (1951) in his work among the Navajo. He noted that within this tribe large extended families tended to conserve Navajo values, exerting a negative influence on assimilation. It is necessary for the counselor to be aware that cultural values can act as barriers to effective cross-cultural counseling (Nobles, 1979).

> Lepley (1944) described values as follows: Descriptively, a man's 'values' may refer to all of his attitudes for or against anything. His values include his preferences and avoidances, his desire-objects and aversion-objects, his pleasure and pain tendencies, his goals, ideals interests and disinterests, what he takes to be right or wrong, good and evil, beautiful and ugly, useful and useless, his approvals and disapprovals, his criteria of taste and standards of judgment and so forth." (p. 2).

> Barry and Wolf (1965) saw a value as "a learned belief so thoroughly internalized that it colors the actions and thoughts of the individual and produces a strong emotional-intellectual response when anything runs counter to it" (p. 40).

> Trimble (1976) sees groups sharing general values that are not radically different values but are simply different in terms of the emphasis placed upon various aspects of a value system shared by other cultures. Perhaps the most accurate definition of value orientation in the behavioral sciences is that of Kluckhohn and Strodtbeck (1961). They define value orientation as "complex but definitely patterned principles, resulting from the transactional interplay of the analytically distinguishable elements of the evaluation process-the cognitive, the affective and the directive elements-which give order and direction to the everflowing stream of human acts and thoughts as these relate to the solution of 'common human problems'" (p. 4).

The above definitions of values refer to the process that defines a very generalized set of goal-oriented expectations. These expectations are based upon a specific foundation inherent within the person's immediate frame of reference. There is much overlapping of such concepts as attitudes, beliefs, ideas and values. An attempted distinction between these concepts is beyond the scope of this study. We can assume that a value orientation reflects an idea of principle intrinsically valuable or desirable (human rather than material) to the individual.

The Case Study Approach of Value Studies

One of the major branches of cultural anthropology is ethnology, which may be defined as the descriptive and comparative study of the world's cultures for the purpose of formulating generalizations about human nature. Ethnology includes the study of techniques, economic organization, kinship associations, government, law, religion, art, folklore, and other aspects of human culture. Ethnologists who emphasize those aspects of culture which most extensively involve relations within and among groups are often referred to as social anthropologists.

Much of the early research on American Indian values was conducted by social anthropologists using the case study approach. Some of the anthropological field studies consisted of long term observations of American Indians in their natural social environment. This involved learning the language and closely sharing their lives in order to penetrate beneath the surface to richer insights and understandings of true cultural values.

Autobiographies, biographies and psychological analyses provided a glimpse of cultural values and individual configurations of behavior (Devereaux, 1951). In addition, American Indians have provided some personal portraits, such as Radin's (1920) account of CRASHING THUNDER, about Indian Life on the plains. SON OF OLD MAN HAT (Dyk, 1938), SUN CHIEF (Simmons, 1942), and SMOKE FROM THEIR FIRES (Ford, 1941) are some of the earliest documents. These life histories reflected social behavior and values which were normative for specific Indian communities or tribes. These personal accounts reflected how a tribal culture and its value patterns were experienced on a personal level.

Life histories, as Kluckhohn (1953) points out, are valuable for the insight they provide into the meaning which social forms have for the members of a given community. Anthropologists are usually interested in more than a specific individuals experiences. They note Sun Chief's sexual attitudes not merely as one individual's way of handling a universal situation, but for what he reveals about that aspect of Hopi culture generally experienced on a personal level. Therefore, it is important to accumulate personal documents from a number of people who occupy different statuses in a particular Indian community.

Another case study, PATTERNS OF CULTURE (Benedict, 1934), compared cultural values of the Indians of the Great Plains with the values of the Pueblo of the Southwest. According to Benedict, the Plains Indians revealed a Dionysian quality, i.e. pressing toward excess in order to achieve a certain psychological state. The Pueblo, in contrast, exhibited an Appollonian quality, meaning they distrusted excess, preferred the middle ground, and avoided disruptive psychological states. Benedict saw the Plains Indians, in response to death, giving way to uninhibited grief, prolonging mourning and some people mutilating their bodies to properly express grief. The Pueblos sought to make as little of the sorrowful event as possible. Benedict saw the Pueblos as valuing the mild-mannered and affable man who acts in a moderate manner in contrast to the grandiose or spectacular ways of the Plains Indian.

Honigmann (1949), in his study of the Kaska, viewed the values of a culture as part of the process of social change. His findings suggest an "ethos" of strong emotional constraint and inhibition of emotional expression in interpersonal relations. Other case studies among Cherokees and Sioux have identified conservative emotional patterns, unconscious persistency and generosity (Gulick, 1960; Meekel, 1936).

Aberle (1951), in a psychosocial analysis of the Hopi, identified those values that make up the ideal person. These values included strength, wisdom, self-control, poise, tranquility, obedience to the law, cooperation, unselfishness, responsibility and kindness. Bryde (1972) developed a list of cultural regularities among the Sioux, which included present time orientation, lack of time consciousness, generosity, respect for age and cooperation. His data was collected from interviews with Sioux elders over a 23 year span. Zintz (1963) studied the values of the Pueblos from reports from school teachers of Pueblo and Anglo-American children. He found the Pueblo preferring a harmony with nature and present time orientation. A comparison of Bryde's and Zintz' case studies reveals a common dimension of agreement. There apparently exists an area of general value orientation which is preferred by many Indian tribal groups.

Hallowell (1951) found a persistence of personality and cultural values among the Ojibwa, independent of the degree of assimilation. Using Rorschach protocols of 217 adult subjects aged 16 through 80 years, he compared three groups of Ojibwas. Group 1 were the least acculturated. His data were collected in 1932 when none of these subjects spoke English. Group II were more acculturated, all were Christianized and no native songs were sung. In addition, no traditional religious Indian ceremonies were performed. Group III were highly acculturated. Practically all spoke English fluently. The data were collected in 1932, 1946 and 1950. In addition, Hallowell compared the accounts of observers who had the most intimate contacts with the tribe in the seventeenth and eighteenth centuries with his data. From the standpoint of behavior, one of the significant features of their culture was the absence of any institutionalized development which brought organized social sanctions to bear upon the individual. They were chiefless, courtless and without jails. The personality structure was highly introverted. It functioned in terms of internalized controls; individuals felt the full brunt of responsibility for their own acts. Sickness and misfortune were thought to be the penalty for wrong doing and experiences of this sort provided the occasion for deep feelings of guilt.

He noted a surface amiability and emotional restraint, tinged with latent suspicion and anxiety. The most striking fact in his findings was the continuity of the acculturation. He found a persistent core of traits which can be identified as Ojibwa, whether they spoke

English, were racially mixed, wore different style of clothing or had different occupations. He found the subjects to be friendly but cautious in interpersonal relationships, possessing a high degree of emotional restraint, highly introverted and having strong beliefs in the supernatural. Day (1975) found similar results in a longitudinal study of Apache subjects using the Rorschach instrument.

These case studies of American Indian tribes have contributed much to the study of cultural values, even though the tribes studied were a small fraction of the total American Indian population.

Comparative Value Studies of American Indians and Anglo-Americans

Early studies have focused on one tribe or similarities and differences between several tribes or tribal groups using the case study approach. The last 25 years has produced cross-cultural studies with a focus on value differences between American Indian and Anglo-American populations.

One of the earliest comparative studies was conducted by Bennett (1946). His study, which compared Zuni and adjacent Pueblo cultures, found cooperation and peaceableness being highly valued by both groups.

One study of six tribal groups was conducted in 1941 in a cooperative venture between the University of Chicago and the United States Office of Indian Affairs (Havighurst & Neugarten, 1955). The purpose was to examine the development of Indian children under the impact of Anglo-American society. The project was conducted by psychologists, psychiatrists, public administrators, linguists and other specialists. The tribal groups for which monographs of findings have been published are the Hopi (Joseph & Thompson, 1944), Sioux (Macgregor, 1946), Papago (Chesky, Joseph & Spicer, 1949), Zuni (Leighton & Adair, 1966) and Navajo (Leighton & Kluckhohn, 1947). A major finding was "that a program of administration which was oriented primarily to assimilate the Indians into the general American population was highly detrimental to the welfare of Indian Communities and Indian personality" (Honigmann, 1961, p. 137).

Other researchers have conducted cross-cultural studies comparing American Indian and Anglo-American values. Kluckhohn and Strodtbeck (1961) narrowed universal value perspectives down to four categories: man/nature, time, activity and relational orientation. This study examined value orientations in five different cultural communities of the American Southwest: Spanish-American, Mormon, Texan, Zuni and Navajo. The authors' goal was to test the assumption that existential and evaluative beliefs are interrelated and may meaningfully differentiate various cultures. Standardized interview schedules were administered to samples of twenty-five individuals from each community. According to the authors, their work demonstrated that it is possible to study the value orientation of a culture through the testing of individuals. The value orientations that were measured through the interview schedule reflected patterns of family organization, economic activities, religious beliefs and rituals, political behavior, attitudes toward education, and intellectual and aesthetic interests as determined independently by anthropologists who were experts on each culture. The existential or general beliefs were seen as influencing concrete choices in everyday life.

In general, the results confirmed the predictions made by the authors: within-culture regularities and between-culture differences emerged. The outstanding results were that Spanish-Americans preferred a Present time orientation, the Being alternative of the activity orientation, and the Subjugated-to-Nature position on the man-nature orientation. Mormons and Texans presented similar value patterns. Both were high on the Doing orientation, but Mormons were slightly higher. The Mormons gave a somewhat lesser emphasis than the Texans to the Individualistic orientation. They were less favorably disposed to the Mastery-over-Nature as opposed to the Harmony-with-Nature alternative of the man-nature orientation. Finally, the Mormons showed a slightly greater tendency than the Texans to choose the Past alternative of the time orientation over the Present alternative. The Zuni exhibited a strong preference for the Doing alternative of the activity orientation, and for the Mastery-over-Nature position of the man/nature orientation. The Navaho showed a preference for the Present alternative of the time orientation, the Harmony-with-Nature alternative of the man/nature orientation, and the Doing alternative of the activity orientation.

Recent value studies of American Indian subjects of other tribes tend to support the findings of Kluckhohn for the sample of Navaho subjects in time orientation (Bryde, 1972; Culbertson, 1977; Zintz, 1963).

Case studies by Bryde (1972) and Zintz (1963 mentioned earlier compared Anglo-American values with the Sioux and Pueblo values, finding similar results to those reported by Kluckhohn and Strodtbeck (1961). A common dimension of agreement was found in values such as Harmony with Nature, Present time orientation, group consensus and cooperation.

Culbertson (1977), using the Kluckhohn questionnaire, compared 14 Indian and 15 non-Indian management students from Southeast Alaska. The sample was non-random. He found no significant differences between the two groups in their orientations toward the man-nature problem. Both groups reflected a Harmony-with-Nature orientation. No significant difference in time orientation between the two groups was found. Both preferred Present time orientation. In the activity category, he found Indians preferring a Doing orientation as opposed to a Being orientation. Overall, he found no significant cultural value differences between the Indian and non-Indian subjects. The Anglo-Americans in his study revealed a movement toward Indian values in time and man-nature categories, indicating a reverse assimilation process taking place.

Ryan (1976) compared 13 male American Indian counselors, 12 female American Indian counselors, 13 male non-Indian counselors and 12 female non-Indian counselors using the Allport, Vernon, Lindzey Study of Values. Variables studied were: achievement, aggression, affiliation understanding, autonomy, endurance, nurturance, economic, play, order, social recognition and dominance. The greatest differences between ethnic groups were found in achievement, affiliation, play, understanding and economic values. Similar findings for both ethnic groups were found in (non) aggression, autonomy, endurance, order, nurturance and social recognition.

Trimble (1976) conducted an exploratory study among 245 Indian and non-Indian high school students in Oklahoma. Using a sentence-completion type instrument, information was elicited in five areas of behavior: achievement, interpersonal relations, authority, aggression and anxiety. Results supported the hypothesis that Indian values differ qualitatively from those of non-Indians, and do correspond with those generally believed to be indicative of the American Indian in general. A significant finding of this study was the degree of value persistence in spite of close contact with non-Indians and a strong influence of the Anglo culture.

Tefft (1967) administered the Kluckhohn questionnaire to 229 white, 36 Arapaho and 45 Shoshone high school students living on or near the Wind River reservation in Wyoming. The data collected showed all three groups preferring individualism over collateral or lineal in the relational category. The Shoshone group reported a preference for future time orientation over present time orientation. The white group preferred future time orientation over present time orientation. The data suggested that on the majority of problem items, the preferred value orientations of the three groups were similar. Tefft attributed these findings to increased culture contact with the dominant culture.

Lewis (1980) conducted a comparative study of 37 American Indian and 40 non-Indian social work graduate students on attitudes toward leadership. The student sample was non-random. A questionnaire was developed from a number of existing questionnaires and administered to the students. Items selected addressed: 1. the kind of person a leader should be, 2. skills a leader should possess, and 3. relative importance of these two general sets of descriptions. Findings revealed that 76% of the Indians believed that kind of person a leader is, was of greater importance than skills or knowledge. The non-Indians reported just the opposite (66%). This difference was statistically significant (Chi square = 9.83, p < .01 df). This difference in criteria for leadership selection was consistent with the study findings on leadership qualities and leader behavior.

The findings were as follows:

1.   Words such as ambition tended to be avoided by Indians.
2.   The category of spiritual leader was rated very high by Indians.
3.   The American Indian students were very concerned with choosing "not the person" but the quality of the person's values.
4.   The Indian students thought the leader should be more person-oriented and less task-oriented.

In general the American Indian students usually suppressed authoritarian style and agressive leadership behavior in contrast to Anglo-American students. Schusky (1970), comparing Sioux and Anglo-Americans, found similar results. He found Anglo-Americans to be much more aggressive and individualistic than the Lower Brule Sioux.

Other studies in the field of education have compared Anglo-American values with the values of elementary and secondary grade school Indian students, but here, again, involving only one or two tribal groups.

Franklyn (1974) conducted a study with randomly selected 9th grade Indian and non-Indian students. An alienation questionnaire was administered to 54 Indian and 54 non-Indian subjects. Data were analyzed by means of t-tests, as well as by analysis of variance and co-variance techniques. A significant difference was reported between the two groups. The findings indicate that the Indian students, more than their non-Indian counterparts, believe that socially unapproved behaviors are justifiable to achieve the important goals and values stressed in the school setting.

Essentially, the Indian life and culture have been uprooted and are now required to serve a new set of institutional norms. It may be that some of the values of these institutions are rejected because they represent the subjection of cultural values to the requirements of the institution. These students may desire a high school education but do not value the rules of competition.

Guilmet (1979) compared Navaho and Caucasian mothers of elementary school children in a non-random sample to test the hypothesis that Navaho mothers displayed a dislike for intense speech interaction and physical behavior in children in classroom situations compared to Caucasian mothers. Using videotapes, seven significant differences (at the .05 probability level) occurred in the responses. The study took place in Los Angeles, California with 23 Navaho and 24 Caucasian mothers. The Caucasian mothers were heavily connected to the university while the Navaho mothers were not. The hypothesis was supported by the study. The Navaho mothers displayed a dislike for intense speech and physical behavior in the classroom.

Miller (1973) compared Blackfeet Indian children to Anglo-American children in games of competition. Two groups of 24 boys from each ethnic group selected from grades 2 and 3 were engaged in competitive games. Analysis of variance at the .01 level of probability indicated significant differences between the two groups. While children engaged in competition even when it was maladaptable to do so, while Blackfeet children cooperated rather than competed. Though the differences were statistically significant they were not dramatic. Similar studies conducted in elementary and secondary schools support these results (Arthur, 1944; Youngman, 1974; Zentner, 1963).

The author compared 36 Anglo-American and 36 American Indian female social workers at the masters level using Kluckhohn's Value Schedule. The samples were randomly selected from the membership of national organizations. Significant differences emerged in the categories of time, relational and man/nature. The study revealed a shift in value orientation of Anglo-Americans toward American Indian values when compared to previous comparative studies. American Indians preferred a profile of Being in activity, Collateral in relational orientation, a Present time orientation and a Harmony-with-Nature man/nature orientation. This Indian sample was drawn from 28 different tribes listed in Table II.

TABLE III

Tribes Represented in the American Indian Sample

1. Apache
2. Blackfeet
3. Chippewa
4. Cree
5. Cherokee
6. Choctaw
7. Colville
8. Flathead
9. Hopi
10. Hidatsa
11. Klamath
12. Lakota
13. Laguna
14. Mandan
15. Mohawk
16. Miwok
17. Muckleshoot
18. Navajo
19. Nez Perce
20. Otoe
21. Potawatomi
22. Quinault
23. Sauk
24. Salish
25. Washoe
26. Yakima
27. Yaqui
28. Yurok

General Assessment and Summary

United States anthropologists have conducted practically all of the value studies involving American Indians. Researchers during the last decade have included psychologists and representatives of other disciplines.

Almost sixty years of field work have produced studies on a portion of the American Indian population. A few cultures are well represented in the literature. The Southwest has been well studied, but many tribes have not received the attention give to the Navajo and the Hopi. For example, Southwest groups such as the Papago and Apache have received little attention in the research. California, the Great Basin and the North Pacific Coast have been studied recently by a few researchers. In the far North and Plains areas the focus has been on the Sioux and Ojibwa-Chippewa communities. Alaska tribes have received some attention recently. The New York Iroquois has been intensively utilized for research as well as the Iroquoian-speaking Cherokee Indians of North Carolina, (Gulick, 1960; Holzinger, 1961).

Though spotty coverage has been accomplished with respect to value studies on American Indians, enough data have been collected to begin to develop wider generalization and comparisons.

A number of reports, including Honigmann (1961), suggest that a high degree of psychological homogeneity based on common values characterize the behavior of the American Indian. David and Spindler (1957), as a result of assembling a portion of the available data, found a commonality in that American Indians, considered as a separate ethnic population without regard to individual differences, valued the following characteristics: non-demonstrative emotionality, the autonomy of the individual, an ability to endure deprivation, bravery, a proclivity for practical joking and a dependence on super-natural powers.

Most of the studies conducted thus far reveal more differences than similarities in values between Anglo-American and American Indian subjects. A variety of instruments have been used, including projective as well as survey instruments and interview techniques.

It is evident from these studies that a preference in core values of American Indians have persisted for a number of years. The literature substantiates that American Indians resist assimilation into the dominant Anglo-American society. Most Indians have persisted in their desire to maintain their tribal and community organizations and to accept only those aspects of Anglo culture that are found useful (Driver, 1961). This self-imposed segregation for Indians is largely responsible for the persistence of residuals of basic cultural values among tribes for centuries.

AMERICAN INDIAN VALUES

The following value orientations were those most preferred in the survey of the literature.

Activity Orientation

The American Indian prefers a Being orientation over a Doing orientation. This implies that intrinsic worth of the individual is more important than education, status, power and wealth. Explanation and predictions regarding American Indians can be made about important aspects of the mother-child relationship based upon these findings. For example a mother of American Indian ancestry will usually be more accepting of her child for what he or she is rather than for what the child can accomplish as compared to the performance of siblings or the children in other families of a locally circumscribed group. This may be one of the reasons that American Indians do not put pressure on their children to excel in the educational system.

American Indians are more likely to be more interested in the quality of life than the accumulation of goods. Their activities reflect a relaxed way of life with little emphasis on saving money or the necessity of buying cars or clothing to impress others. Indians would rather work less hours and have more time to relax and enjoy their family and friends than to work long hours in order to buy automobiles or fancy homes.

In the spiritual realm, the path of life for American Indians must have meaning. There is a purpose for suffering and in dying. But no one can tell another what this purpose is. Each must find out for one's self, and must accept the responsibility that his/her answer prescribes.

This meaning in life is a primary force and not an instinctual drive. It is unique and must be fulfilled by the person themself, only then does it become significant. People are always free to make choices between fulfilling a meaningful potentiality or of passing it by.

A Being philosophy is of little value politically. This is one of the main reasons why American Indians have never gained political power in the United States. Political power and the activities leading up to its achievement require a Doing philosophy. Historically, few American Indians have been elected to congress in the last 200 years.

A Being philosophy is portrayed most dramatically in the dances and creative works of American Indians. Poetry and paintings have captured the peace and tranquility which stems from a Being philosophy of life. Even the language and non-verbal communication reflect serenity and tranquility as first fruits of this orientation.

In all spheres of Indian life harmony and peace, as we have seen, was mandatory--a condition of nature itself. The turbulence and velocity of change in the West which has epitomized the destiny of the nineteenth and twentieth centuries was unknown among Indians. Such drastic change was not typical of the lives of tribal people to disrupt or fundamentally alter their worldview.

Relational Orientation

American Indians would rather cooperate rather than compete. According to the value surveys, Indians prefer a Collateral orientation in the relational category. A Collateral orientation places the welfare of the group first. Many American Indian societies are focused upon an extended series of patterned kin reciprocities. About the most unfavorable moral judgment an Indian can pass on another person is to say "he acts as if he didn't have any relatives".

It is through relationships that American Indians comprehend themselves. Such relationships are portrayed by elaborations of languages and ritual activities. The Indian is spiritually interdependent upon the language, folk history, ritualism, and geographical sacredness of his or her whole people. The relatedness of the individual and the tribe extends outward beyond the family to include the entire world. Nothing exists in isolation. Individualism does not presuppose autonomy, alienation or isolation. Freedom is not the right to express yourself but the far more fundamental right to be yourself.

One of the most significant features of Indian tribal custom is the giving of individuated names. These names are representative of personal qualities, uncommon abilities, visionary experiences and peak experiences. This name validates his/her uniqueness.

Individualism is a highly valued concept in American life. Individualism conceptualizes dynamism and ambitiousness of the free person. If an American did not achieve the successful dream it was clearly the individual's own fault. Though originally it denoted equality, the consensus of today is that some people are more equal than others. In addition the criteria for measuring success is undergoing close scrutiny as people search for other more meaningful criteria than material goods as evidence of success.

This does not mean that the "individual" is nonexistent among Indian communities nor that each person cannot possess access to sacredness; but it does mean that the highly individuated egocentricity of the Western soul is alien to the majority of Indians.

American Indians tend to be tribal or collateral rather than idiosyncratic in their psychology. For instance, most North American tribes possess what must be called a "communal soul" in comparison with the Western precept of the soul as personal property. Among the Iroquoian people the power that vivifies the tribe is called the Orenda; and it is this force which animates the members of the tribe. People enrich the power that gives them life, and then they pass out of existence. What remains is the tribe; the Orenda.

The nature of authority patterns stem from the relational orientation. Indian people place a high value on the welfare of the extended family and this family loyalty is sometimes mistaken for dependency. A loyalty to family and group consensus is sometimes seen as blocking the individuation process as conceptualized by some Anglo-American social workers and human service personnel.

Economically, Indians are known for sharing their food and goods with their relative and friends. Most Indian tribes originally shared a communal lifestyle. Residuals of this system still exist. Generosity and cooperation are qualities of high value within the Collateral value orientation.

Time Orientation

Based upon the research studies of the last few decades, American Indians prefer a Present time orientation. The focus of a Present time orientation is on living from day to day and experiencing life as it comes. It demonstrates an appreciation for the here and now with little focus or confidence in the future. Indians are not clock watchers in their domestic life. They tend to be relaxed and unhurried in their daily tasks. This Present time perspective requires an awareness and appreciation of the moment, a characteristic lacking in Western society. The future orientation of the Western world deprives the individual of enjoying the present. Many Westerners sacrifice the present for dreams of a better tomorrow which they never live to experience.

Most American Indians view time as simultaneously an illusion and a much broader notion than it is commonly thought of. That is, what is sensed as time is largely a human construct, and only a shadow of what time "really" is.

Also, a second theme of American Indian time orientation is that the future (as well as the past) is not as relevant to one's life purpose, and to the actions needed to fulfill that purpose, as is commonly supposed. Most preoccupation with the future (planning, insurance, stockpiling possessions, etc.) arises out of insecurities, which come in turn from fears that one will lose what one thinks one needs for physical survival, comfort, happiness or an appropriate sense of identity. These fears are all ungrounded and losses occur only because fear is present. This philosophy stresses the illusory nature of time as an element of human existence.

In harmony with this orientation is another basic part of American Indian philosophy which reflects an existential worldview. This view is that every person has a very high degree of control over his or her own future. Through one's thoughts, attitudes and beliefs, one shapes the perceptions through which one interfaces with reality. Each person literally "creates" individually and collectively, and at various levels, the entire life situation in which one finds one self. Thus the future is never fully determined.

In summary, Time is not what one thinks it is, the present is all one has, the future is not as important as it seems to be (to Westerners), many futures exist from which one can make choices and people have a great amount of control over their own futures. In short, one's own precognitive abilities may be applied to help self or others to relate constructively to one's ow future.

Man/Nature Orientation

American Indians prefer a Harmony with Nature orientation. The aim is to maintain "balance" or "harmony" among the various aspects of the universe.

American Indian thought is inclined to employ spatial metaphors to describe the unity of everything in the cosmos. "Once this spiritual vision of the cosmos is recognized" according to historian L. Donald Hughes "the Indian attitude toward the land itself becomes understandable. The land was the gift of the domain of powerful beings. Certain locations, such as mountains and lakes, served as especially important points of contact with these spirits or forces. The Indian's relationship to the world is structured by sacred geography. Holy people tend to treat the human mind, the human body, and the whole world of nature as a single integrated organism. The Indian has a very strong and pervasive sense of place, and does not look at space as a possession. The land belongs to the past and the future, and it will be the home of the children and their children after them" (Hughes, 1977, p. 2-13).

According to the astronomer Ray Williamson the sacredness of space is not limited in the Indian mentality to the relation of place to earthly directions, but is accurately related to heavenly movement. The castle of the Anasaza (a Navajo term meaning "the ancient ones" - the ancestors of the Pueblo people of today) incorporated two special sighting holes, into the walls, one aligned to the summer solstice sunset on June 21, the other to the winter solstice sunset on December 21. In addition, they designed the outside doorway of the castle so that its jambs align to sunset on the two equinoxes (roughly March 21 and September 21), when day equals night in length. It is believed that the Pueblo people seven hundred years ago may have employed a precise spatially oriented calendar for planting, harvesting, and ritual observances (Williamson, 1978, p. 78-85).

The Indian experience of space is not linear; it does not fit into the patterns so common in Western spatial orientation. The tribal person knows space experientially (Highwater, 1981).

For American Indians worship is dance. The idea that spirituality can be associated with the body is extremely remote from the white man's belief in the dichotomy of mind and body, spirit and flesh...To most non-Indians dancing is a form of mindless amusement. Dance has been detested by church and synagogue...The Indian concept of harmony among all thingsis so alien to the West that Westerners cannot conceive of a spiritual conviction that is communicated through dance...Indians have often stated that dancing is "the breath of life" made visible. This concept of the breath of life is discovered everywhere in the unique spiritual world of Indians; in the ceremonial stem of the sacred pipe, in th heart line of animals imprinted on pottery, in the rites of inhaling the first light of day and the conferring of blessing by exhaling into the hands of a devotee. All these symbolic images and gestures are associated with the wind and with the breathing of the living cosmos-the visible motion of the power that invests everything in existence (Highwater, 1981, p. 135-136).

Song, rhythm, dance and motion are central to Indian culture. It is a theme that runs elaborately through every Indian tradition regardless of the diversity among the tribes. "The perfectly coordinated, lavishly expressive body of the ritual dancer is different from the prim, rather stiff, and fashionably styled body of the ballet dancer." (Highwater, 1981, p. 149). Dancing in a natural way is so profoundly simple, and that is what makes it so difficult for modern Western people to comprehend.

Primal people have little concern or faith in the materialism that imposes mind/brain and soul/body dichotomies...Life is holistic, and not imprisoned in a linear universe with its unthinkable Copernican gears moving some pathetic, calculated clock by which only civilized Westerners are supposed to be able to tell the correct time...

Both Western and tribal dancers, however, seem to have something in common; they are both aliens standing outside the value systems of the now dominant culture" (Highwater 1981, p. 150-151).

The changes in viewpoint stem from a reappraisal of Western sex roles, of the worship of materialism and of the rampant alienation from self experienced by the white man's attitude toward himself and his body.

The American Indian understands that he/she is linked intimately with the earth in a network of rights and responsibilities. The earth is viewed as the mother and the sky as the father. The land then is sacred, encompassing a spiritual dimension dating back to the Ice Age. There is no thought of anything other than living in harmony with nature.

Sections of this Chapter has been reprinted by permission from: Highwater, J. PRIMAL MIND: VISION AND REALITY IN INDIAN AMERICA (New York, Harper Collins) 1981.

WESTERN SPIRITUAL HUNGER

American society is in the process of transformation. The historian, Arnold Toynbee, stated that it is a characteristic of all civilizations in their declining days that they look to foreign cultures for their new philosophies of life. So it is today that the dominant society is looking to American Indian philosophy as well as others for guidance and direction. Modern society is struggling with a metaphysical crisis of gigantic proportion. A spiritual vacuum exists. The central problem stems from an obsession with technology and materialism.

There is a resurgence of interest in the United States and Europe in the literature and legends of American Indians. It appears that the Western world is seeking something of substance to cling to as the emptiness of materialism settles in. Indian mythology is essentially an autobiography of a people. The symbols and myths of a culture exert a force beyond the consciousness of a people and exist indefinitely. The interpretation of the legends and myths of American Indians gives the key to the inner history of a spiritual and humble people. Perhaps it is this spirituality found in American Indian legends which is satisfying a spiritual hunger for Westerners.

Fundamentally the continuity in history does not consist of the external forms of civilization or in events but in the forces that are active in the minds, hearts and souls of people. Toynbee states that while the outer structure of a civilization breaks apart when it "dies", something yet lives on.

Historically the Rainbow has been the symbol of the beginning of a new era and the end of a stormy, turbulent period, as with Noah and the flood in bible days. It appears that the people in many parts of the world are undergoing change and transformation and looking for a new rainbow.

Marilyn Ferguson says there are four basic ways in which we change. The easiest of these is called change by exception. Old beliefs remain intact but a handful of anomalies are tolerated. Then there is incremental change which occurs bit by bit and the person is not aware of having changed. Then there is pendulum change, the abandonment of one closed and certain system for another. The hawk becomes a dove. Pendulum change fails to integrate what was right with the old and fails to discriminate the value of the new from its overstatements. Pendulum change rejects its own prior existence, going from one kind of half-knowing to another. Last, there is paradigm change-transformation. It is the fourth dimension of change: the new perspective, the insight that allows the information to come together in a new form or structure. It refines and integrates. In many ways it is the most challenging kind of change because it relinquishes certainty. It allows for different interpretations from different perspectives at different times.

Change itself changes, just as in nature, evolution evolves from a simple to a complex process. Paradigm change is not a simple linear effect. It is a sudden shift of pattern, a spiral, and sometimes a cataclysm. When one wakes up to the alteration of ones own awareness one augments change. Synthesis builds on synthesis.

Before change occurs people are caught between two different evolutionary mechanisms: denial and transformation. The capacity for denial is an example of the body's sometimes short-sighted vision. Rather than experiencing and transforming pain, conflict and fear, one often diverts or dampens them with a kind of hypnotic denial. The result is that the real alienation in present time is not from society but from self. Conflict, pain, tension, fear, paradox...these are transformations trying to happen. Once a person confronts them, the transformative process begins.

The Western dream of a two car garage, a house in the suburbs and a swimming pool does not satisfy the soul. The Westerner has been seeking a materialistic pot of gold at the end of the rainbow. The Indian philosophy (which many Indians have lost or traded for Western ideas) teaches that the path (goal) of life is the process of life itself. The process of life is an adventure of learning and experiencing reality as a part of nature and the cosmos. This process is unique for each person. Learning and knowledge are not permanent, but experienced for a brief instant. Learning is never what one expects and every step is a new task that begins in infancy and continues until death.

American Indian philosophy teaches that people are never clear about their goals and objectives in the beginning because their purpose is faulty and their intent is vague. The young and inexperienced hope for rewards that will never materialize because they do not understand the hardships of true learning. The path of life must and will proceed regardless of whether one is capable of finding satisfaction and personal fulfillment in making one' life choices.

The path then is an existential concept which reflects the quality and purpose of life for each person. The path cannot be chosen for another. Each person must look for inward guidance in this selection and will ultimately know if he/she is on the right path or not.

American Indian philosophy of enlightenment is a state of peace and tranquility resulting from harmony of systems within and without the person. This harmony extends to living in harmony with other people and all of the Great Spirit's creation.

REFERENCES

Aberle, D.F. (1951). The psychosocial analysis of a Hopi life history. COMPARATIVE PSYCHOLOGY MONOGRAPHS, 21 (1), 80-138.

Albert, E.M. (1963). Conflict and change in American Values. ETHICS, October, 1963, LXXIV, 2, 20.

Arthur, G. (1944). An experience in examining an Indian twelfth grade group with the multiphasic personality inventory. MENTAL HYGIENE, 28, 253-250.

Bachtold, L.M. & Eckvall, K.L. (1978). Current value orientations of American Indians in Northern California: The Hupa. JOURNAL OF CROSS-CULTURAL PSYCHOLOGY. 9 (3) 367-375.

Barry, R. & Wolf, B. (1965). MOTIVES, VALUES AND REALITIES. New York: Teacher College Press, Teachers College, Columbia University, p. 40.

Benedict, R. (1934). PATTERNS OF CULTURE. Boston: Houghton Mifflin.

Bennet, J. (1946). The interpretation of Pueblo culture: a question of values. SOUTHWESTERN JOURNAL OF ANTHROPOLOGY, 2: 361-374.

Bryde, J.F. (1972). INDIAN STUDENTS AND GUIDANCE. Boston: Houghton Mifflin.

Culbertson, H.J. (1977). Values and behaviors: An exploratory study of differences between Indians and non-Indians. (Doctoral dissertation, University of Washington, 1977). DISSERTATION ABSTRACTS INTERNATIONAL, 38 (6-A) 3596. (University Microfilms No. 77-26, 809).

Day, R., Boyer, L.B., & Devos, G.A. (1975). Two styles of ego development: a cross-cultural longitudinal comparison of Apache and Anglo school children. ETHOS, 3 (3), 345-380.

Devereaux, G. (1951).   REALITY AND DREAM. New York: International Universities Press.

Driver, H.E. (1961). INDIANS OF NORTH AMERICA. Chicago: University of Chicago Press.

Dyk, W. (1938). SON OF OLD MAN HAT. New York, Harcourt, Brace & Co.

English, H.B., & English, A.C. (1958). A COMPREHENSIVE DICTIONARY OF PSYCHOLOGICAL AND PSYCHOANALYTICAL TERMS: A GUIDE TO USAGE. New York: David McKay Co.

Ferguson, Marilyn (1980). THE AQUARIAN CONSPIRACY. J.P. Tarcher, Inc., Los Angeles.

Ford, C.S. (1941). SMOKE FROM THEIR FIRES. New Haven: Yale University Press.

Franklyn, G.J. (1974). Alienation and achievement among Indian-Metis and non-Indian in the Mackenzie district of the Northwest territories. ALBERT JOURNAL OF EDUCATIONAL RESEARCH, June, 1974, 20 (2), 157-169.

Guilment, G.M. (1979). Maternal perceptions of urban Navajo and Caucasian children's classroom behavior. HUMAN ORGANIZATION, Spring 1979, 38 (1), 87-91.

Gulick, J. (1960). CHEROKEES AT THE CROSSROADS. Chapel Hill, North Carolina: Institute for Research in Social Sciences, 1960.

Hallowell, A.I. (1951). The use of projective techniques in the study of the socio-psychological aspects of acculturation. JOURNAL OF PROJECTIVE TECHNIQUES, 15, 27-44.

Havighurst, R.J. & Neugarten, B.L. AMERICAN INDIAN AND WHITE CHILDREN: A SOCIOPSYCHOLOGICAL INVESTIGATION. Chicago: University of Chicago Press.

Highwater, Jamake (1981). THE PRIMAL MIND: VISION AND REALITY IN INDIAN AMERICA. New York, Harper Row.

Holzinger, C.H. (1961). Some observations on the persistence of aboriginal Cherokee personality traits. In W.N. Fenton & J. Gulick (Eds.), SYMPOSIUM ON CHEROKEE AND IROQUOIS CULTURE. Bureau of American Ethnology, Bulletin 180.

Honigmann, J. (1949). CULTURE AND ETHOS OF KASHA SOCIETY. Yale University Publications in Anthropology.

Honigmann, J. (1961). North America. In F. Hsu (Eds.), PSYCHOLOGICAL ANTHROPOLOGY. Homewood, Illinois: Dorsey Press.

Hughes, J. Donald (1977). "Forest Indians: The Holy Occupation". ENVIRONMENTAL REVIEW February 2-13.

Joseph, A., Spicer, R. & Chesky, J. (1949). THE DESERT PEOPLE: A STUDY OF THE PAPAGO INDIANS OF SOUTHERN ARIZONA. Chicago, University of Chicago Press.

Kluckhohn, C. (1954). Southwestern studies of culture and personality. AMERICAN ANTHROPOLOGIST, 56, 685-697.

Kluckhohn, F.R. (1953). Dominant and variant value orientations. In C. Kluckhohn & H.A. Murray (Eds.). PERSONALITY IN NATURE, SOCIETY AND CULTURE. New York: Alfred A. Knopf.

Kluckhohn, F.R. (1953). Dominant and variant value orientations. In C. Kluckhohn & H.A. Murray (Eds.). PERSONALITY IN NATURE, SOCIETY AND CULTURE. New York: Alfred A. Knopf.

Leighton, D.C. & Adair, J. (1966). PEOPLE OF THE MIDDLE PLACE. New Haven: Behavior Science Monographs.

Leighton, D.C. & Kluckhohn, C. (1947). CHILDREN OF THE PEOPLE. Cambridge, Harvard University Press.

Lepley, R. (1944). VERIFIABILITY OF VALUE. New York: Columbia University Press.

Lewis, R.G. & Ginerich, W. (1980). Leadership characteristics: Views of Indians non-Indian students. SOCIAL CASEWORK, October 1980.

Macgregor, G. (1946). WARRIORS WITHOUT WEAPONS. Chicago: University of Chicago Press.

Meekel, H.S. (1936). THE ECONOMY OF A MODERN TETON DAKOTA COMMUNITY. New Haven Connecticut: Yale University Press.

Miller, G. (1973). Integration and acculturation of cooperative behavior among Blackfeet Indian and non-Indian Canadian children. JOURNAL OF CROSS-CULTURAL PSYCHOLOGY, September, 1973, 4, 374-380.

Nobles, W.W. (1979). The right of culture: A declaration for the provision of culturally sensitive mental health services and the issue of protected status. In MULTI-CULTURAL ISSUES IN MENTAL HEALTH SERVICES. California: Department of Mental Health, pp. 139-140.

REPORT OF THE PRESIDENT'S COMMISSION ON MENTAL HEALTH (1979). Washington, DC: U.S. Government Printing Office.

Radin, P. (1920). The autobiography of a Winnebago Indian. University of California, PUBLICATIONS IN AMERICAN ARCHAEOLOGY AND ETHNOLOGY, 16, 381-473.

Ryan, L.M.J. (1976). A study of personality traits and values of American Indian and non-American Indian counselors trained at the University of South Dakota. (Doctoral dissertation, University of South Dakota, 1976). DISSERTATION ABSTRACTS INTERNATIONAL, 37 (06-A), 3427. (University Microfilms No. 76-24, 521).

Samler, J. (1966). Change in values: A goal in counseling in B.N. Ard (Eds.), COUNSELING AND PSYCHOTHERAPY. Palo Alto, California: Science and Behavior Books, p. 196.

Scheibe, K.E. (1970). BELIEFS AND VALUES. New York: Macmillan Co., The Free Press.

Schusky, E.L. (1970). Culture change and continuity in the Lower Brule Community. In E. Nurge (Eds.), THE MODERN SIOUX: SOCIAL SYSTEMS AND RESERVATION CULTURE. Lincoln: University of Nebraska Press.

Simmons, L. (1942). (Ed.) SUN CHIEF, THE AUTOBIOGRAPHY OF A HOPI INDIAN. New Haven: Yale University Press.

Tefft, S.K. (1967). Anomy, values, and culture change among teen-age Indians: An exploratory study. SOCIOLOGY OF EDUCATION. Spring, p. 145-157.

Thompson, L. & Joseph, A. (1944). THE HOPI WAY. Chicago: University of Chicago Press.

Toynbee, Arnold J. (1962). AMERICA AND THE WORLD REVOLUTION. New York, Oxford University Press.

Trimble, J.E. (1974). The intrusion of western psychological thought on Native American ethos. Paper presented at the Second International Conference of the International Association for Cross-Cultural Psychology, Kingston, Ontario, Canada. August, 1974, (b).

Trimble, J.E. (1976). Value differences among American Indians: Concerns for the concerned counselor. In P. Pederson et al. COUNSELING ACROSS CULTURE. Honolulu: University Press of Hawaii.

Vogt, E. (1951). Navajo Veterans: A study of changing values. PAPERS OF THE PEABODY MUSEUM OF ARCHEOLOGY AND ETHNOLOGY, 41 (no. 1).

Williamson, Ray (1978). "Native Americans were Continent's First Astronomers". THE SMITHSONIAN, October, p. 78-85.

Youngman, G. & Sadonei, J. (1974). Counseling the American Indian. ELEMENTARY SCHOOL GUIDANCE AND COUNSELING. May, 8, 273-277.

Zentner, H. (1963). Value congruence among Indian and non-Indian high school students in southern Alberta. ALBERTA JOURNAL OF EDUCATION RESEARCH, 9, (3), 168-178.

Zintz, M.V. (1963). EDUCATION ACROSS CULTURES. Dubuque, Iowa: William C. Brown & Co.

4. SOCIAL CASEWORK WITH AMERICAN INDIAN POPULATIONS

In general, without regard to either variations among different tribes, individuals within the same tribe or degree of assimilation of individuals or tribes, a growing volume of literature points to differences in basic values between American Indians and the dominant Anglo-American cultures. This text does not attempt to propose why, or identify mechanisms on how this has come about: whether they are passed from generation to generation through traditions and way of life; provide cultural identity; arise because of spiritual beliefs; are unconscious, conscious, developmental, or generic, or even a combination of the host of theoretical explanations thus far proposed. It does point out that in helping American Indian clients, the Anglo-American social worker should be aware of the possibility that differences in basic values could exist which would not only negate the intended assistance, but be the source of cultural conflict through the "imposing" of Anglo values by the unsensitized social worker. Although not exhaustive, examples of some basic value differences which have been found not only to exist, but to be characteristic and wide spread are discussed together with case studies where actual conflicts have been averted through the intervention of workers trained to provide "culturally relevant" services. It is the intent of the author to propagate this type of understanding, suggest methods whereby a difference in value orientation of the client may be identified, and include bibliographies of resource material where further, more specific knowledge may be integrated.

The California Department of Mental Health in its MULTI-CULTURAL ISSUES IN MENTAL HEALTH SERVICES (Nobles, 1979, p. 139) gives the rationale and need for greater understanding of cultural diversity, especially among those who are directly involved in the delivery of social services: "The recognition of culture as a requisite ingredient in the provision of mental health services, requires that one reassess both the notion of culture and the process by which it's expression is guaranteed in this mental health system. A people's culture, in simple terms, is basically the expression of all that

61

constitutes their every day way of life. More specifically, a people's culture is or includes the vast structures of language, behavior, custom, knowledge, symbols, ideas, and values which provide the people with a general design for living and patterns for interpreting reality. The cultural consciousness of a people and their values consistent with it particularly determine or help to define, select, create and re-create what is considered "real", normal, valuable, desirable, appropriate, etc. (and conversely, what is unreal, abnormal, undesirable, inappropriate, etc.) in the people's social milieu, it becomes and is a necessary variable in the formula of mental health services.

Human societies have always been characterized by a richness of cultural types. Unfortunately, however, the natural cultural diversity associated with human societies has been the subject of a dangerous trend toward standardization wherein all cultural diversity is reduced to a single type or pattern. In the world community, the industrialized "Western Pattern" has been decreed as the standard type. In this country the white or Anglo-American type has been similarly decreed as the standard type. The standard type or pattern does, of course, filter through, every aspect of life and, subsequently finds itself being the benchmark for "normality" and therefore, the goal of mental health care. It is not surprising that the mental health system, like all institutions in this society, can be justifiably indicted as being designed to meet only the needs of middle-class educated white Americans. The issue of this declaration is now, however, to explicate the fundamental basis of American institutions.

The purpose of this declaration is to establish in principle and in practice a people's "right of culture" and the implication this inalienable right has for the provision of mental health services. Since a people's culture represents and encompasses their shared, symbolic, systematic, and cumulative ideas, beliefs and knowledge, and, since mental health concerns by definition must be concerned with its "clients" ideas, beliefs, etc., about reality, culture must be or should be viewed as the foundation to any "understanding" of mental wellness and/or illness.

The majority of historical studies, on Indians although justifiably accused of being slanted and tending to stereotype Indians as somehow primitive and inferior, even "savage", have none-the-less contributed to a continued awareness that major differences in ways of life are persistent within the so-called 'melting pot' of the United States. The "Indian philosophy" has been examined by more and more Americans of all ethnic backgrounds as they become less enchanted with the materialism in their surroundings. National concern about ecology and environmental issues has resulted in examining the practices of Native Americans who for centuries lived in harmony with man, animals and nature. From these perspectives, the differences in ways of life can hardly be called 'inferior', and a minimum different. Many of these differences might well necessarily become part of a reverse assimilation process as mankind, including Americans, struggles to overcome his tendency toward self-annihilation through nuclear holocaust.

Indian-ness

Any attempt to define "Indianness' is hopelessly entangled in individual variation and objective interpretation. Rather then, some background on what characteristics the social services client who identifies him/herself as Indian has in common with others similarly self-identified, seems more practical. Understanding traditional Indian values and their potentially conflicting opposites in the non-Indian population is a useful starting point to implementing the objectives of effective social programs which ostensibly are designed to help less fortunate individuals without interfering with that individual's right to self-determination.

Kluckhohn (1961) saw variations in cultural values as an interlocking network of dominant (most preferred) value orientations and variant or substitute value orientations which are both required and permitted. Kluckhohn's theory assumes that there is a limited number of common human problems for which all people at all times must find some solution. while there is variability in the solutions of all problems, these are neither limitless nor random, but fall within a definite range of differentially preferred value orientation, which has been found to be one of the commonalities shared as ethnically characteristic, even to the point of residual influence in assimilated individuals, as best illustrated in a discussion of four 'problems' which Kluckhohn saw as crucial to all human groups.

1. What is the relationship of man to nature?
2. What is the temporal focus of human life?
3. What is the modality of human activity?
4. What is the modality of man's relationship to others?

Those cultures that believe there is little or nothing that can be done to protect themselves from storms or acts of nature are considered, in terms of man-nature orientation, subjugated to nature. The concept of harmony with nature indicates no real separation of man, nature and super-nature. Each is an extension of the other and the concept of wholeness derives from their unity. Mastery over nature is the belief that natural forces are to be overcome. Here, there is an emphasis on technology, e.g. rivers are to be damned for their source of hydroelectric power.

Every society must deal with time problems; all have a temporal focus within their conceptions of the past, the present and future. Future oriented cultures would tend to stress the importance of planning and saving for a better tomorrow, whereas past oriented peoples would cling to the traditional manner in which things had been accomplished historically. Present oriented peoples stress the importance of the here and now.

Differences in human activity orientation are based upon distinctions between being and doing; i.e. man's mode of self-expression in activity. The being orientation, a non-developmental concept, gives preference for spontaneous expression of what is inherent in the human personality, e.g. men feeling sadness might openly shed tears in public. The doing orientation demands activity which results in accomplishments that are measurable by standards external to the individual, e.g. men don't cry, they obtain degrees in higher education <u>proving</u> their worth.

Man's relationship to other men has three subdivisions of orientation: the lineal, the collateral and the individualistic. If the lineal principle is the dominant, the most important group goals are the continuity of the group through time and ordered positional succession, e.g. first son's inheritance. A dominant collateral orientation calls for a primacy of the goals and welfare of laterally extended groups, e.g. support of a clan member residing away from his geographic area of origin. When the individualistic principle is dominant, individual goals have primacy over the goals of specific collateral or lineal groups.

Using cross-cultural studies, several characteristically preferred values, which differ between Anglo-American's and traditional Indian American's have been identified.

Examples are listed in Table IV.

TABLE IV

Preferred Values

ANGLO	ORIENTATION	INDIAN
mastery of nature		harmony with nature
avarice and greedy		beneficial, reasonable
use of resources		use of resources
	NATURE	
private domain		land belongs to all
	TIME	
future oriented		present oriented
planning		impulsive
time awareness		time non-awareness
impatience		patience
saving		giving
emphasis on youth		emphasis & respect for age

ANGLO	ORIENTATION	INDIAN
competitive		cooperative
strong self importance		low self value
aggressive		submissive
guilt		shame
noise		silence

	ACTIVITY	
overstates, over-confident		modest
individuality		anonymity
materialistic		work for present needs
wealth		equality
theoretical		pragmatic
individual emphasis		group, clan emphasis
immediate family		extended family, clan
representative government		face to face government

	RELATIONSHIP	
privacy and use of roominess in living space		compact living in close contact and high indoor space utilization
social coercion		permissiveness

	SPIRITUAL	
skeptical		mystical
logical		intuitive
converts others to religion		respects other's religion
religion-segment of life		religion-way of life

Method of Intervention
(Assessment)

Many college courses in social work methods focus on theories developed by and appropriate for population of West European ancestry, but which many times are irrelevant in working with American Indian clients. The <u>dual perspective</u> has been found to be a valuable beginning step toward the delivery of culturally relevant services to Indian clients (CSWE, 1978).

The dual perspective is a concept that every individual is at the same time part of two systems: the larger system of the dominant society, and the smaller system of the individual's immediate physical and social environment. This conceptual tool describes a very complex process, the complexity stemming from the variety of subsystems within each of the two larger systems. The dual perspective is then, the conscious and systematic process of perceiving, understanding and comparing simultaneously the values, attitudes, and behavior of the larger societal system with those of the client's immediate family and community system. For many minority groups, including American Indians, conflicts grow out of the degree of incongruence between the two systems.

It is necessary that the social worker has specific cultural knowledge of the nurturing environment (immediate, smaller system) of the client and be willing to non-judgmentally view the clients' responses in the context of the particular sociocultural circumstances in which he finds himself. Typical examples of value incongruence which might arise to test the uninitiated Anglo-American social worker's self-awareness and empathy can be hypothetically formulated from the time orientation values of Table IV.

Anglo-Americans, as the world community knows full well, are time conscious: "Clock-watchers". "Time is money". "Promptness is a virtue". Traditional American Indians, on the other hand, place no value on the incremental progression of time. This is carried to the extreme that the more assimilated members of the latter group have coined the term "Indian time" to describe why meetings and social gatherings rarely begin on schedule. It would not be unusual, frowned upon, or in the least bit misinterpreted, if an essential member of a tribal counsel meeting appeared one or two hours after the time appointed for the meeting to begin. With, and without, this information, the Anglo-American reader should now search his own hypothetical mental set to describe his response to the same tribal member: 1) who appears for his 1:45p.m. initial interview at 3:37p.m., or 2) who, after two days has been fired for tardiness from the job it took all week to persuade a local manufacturer to create. Realizing the impact of cultural training on expectation, it would not be unreasonable to expect frustration, or in the rare or experienced social worker, humor at the disregard with which the traditional Indian holds the Anglo-American orientation toward time. The dual perspective allows for viewing these specific situations from the point of view of the Indian client, who may feel similar frustration, or humor, at the Anglo-American time orientation, which to him appears to border on obsession.

The social worker, who by means of the dual perspective, has broadened his understanding of, and sensitivity to, the totality of the life situation of the client group is better able to synthesize the most effective intervention. This perception forces the social worker, who presumably has eliminated bias through awareness of his own attitudes, to answer the question of whether to work with the immediate environment, with the larger dominant environment, with both systems, or whether to intervene at all. In all cases the services built from this perspective are based on the needs of the particular situation.

A distinguishing feature of the professional is the kind of decision he makes. The outcome of a particular course of action in working with a client is dependent on the knowledge of the worker and his assessment of the client's needs. The dual perspective provides a frame of reference for making more effective professional decisions and more accurate assessments.

Existential Model

In alleviating intrapsychic conflicts and emotional problems, the social worker goes beyond assessment. A useful approach in the intervention with these situations is an existential model. This approach to counseling is based on the assumption that the degree of success of the outcome is directly a function of the relationship the social worker establishes with the client.

In this model intervention is a dialogue in the deepest and most genuine sense--an honest exchange between the social worker and the client. The worker is not an insensitive, technical expert who acts on the passive client; rather, they are partners on a journey where neither knows the end. It is the goal that the worker may understand the world of the client from a subjective viewpoint and, at the same time, reveal personal reactions toward the client during the relationship. Both worker and client may be changed by the encounter.

The worker does not rely on a well-developed set of techniques. Instead, he/she focuses on certain themes that are accepted as being part of the "human condition". The central concern is to provide a climate in which the client evaluates his/her past choices and is able to freely choose for himself/herself in the present. The client may see ways in which his existence is limited, but through a common process of incorporating a negative image into his identity has devalued himself. The social worker skilled at existential method helps the client take steps toward liberation by helping the client recreate one's own identity at one's own pace through decisions of one's own choosing.

Application of this modality of intervention is illustrated in the CASE OF JAMES below. Although James is not an actual client, he is a synthesis of many common themes observed by workers serving Indian clients. He has been 'put together' to clarify some of the unclear notions on how to apply the existential concepts.

CASE OF JAMES
Client of Mary, MSW

Introduction to Agency

Mary was contacted by a friend with a concern for a middle aged Indian man who was depressed over the death of his son. Mary realized the traditional American Indian, after generations of dealing with the United States government, has a well-founded and deep-seated mistrust in agencies. She therefore knew that if the man, James, was to be availed of mental health services, outreach intervention would probably be the only way in which this could occur. She made arrangements in her schedule to attempt establishment of this relationship at James' home.

Age	Sex	Ethnicity	Marital Status	Children
52	M	Yakui	Separated	3

Living Situation

James lives with his sister and her three school age children in a rented two bedroom house.

Presenting Problem

James is depressed over the death of his oldest son, who was killed in a car accident while driving under the influence of alcohol. James is also unemployed.

History of Presenting Problem

James was a carpenter until he was laid off, by reason of the new construction slowdown. Shortly after becoming unemployed, his 18 year old son was killed in a one car accident. James had argued with his son earlier the very same day of the accident over the use of the family car.

Recently James has become aware of his loss of self-esteem: the loss of his job and not providing for his family, and his guilt over the death of his son.

Psychosocial History

James is the oldest of six children. His father, deceased, was a Yakui farmer; his mother, a fulltime homemaker. Due to his mother's ill health, James was expected to assume many of the responsibilities of rearing his younger siblings and for maintaining the household.

James left home at age 18 and learned the carpenter trade in western city. At age 30, he met and married his present wife, Anna a woman of the Navajo tribe. Four children were born, the oldest son, and three daughters. He recently separated from his wife since the death of their son.

Worker's Process Commentary

Within a few weeks after the initial visit to James' home, the social worker, Mary, was able to assist James in finding a new job as a maintenance man in a large hospital. With the income problem alleviated, James was now interested in working through his grief over the death of his son.

James had become involved with the resources and services of Mary's agency, through her outreach efforts and friendly visits.

The critical aspect of James' therapy was that moment of recognition where he realized he had a choice to make in how he would handle this loss. He could cling to it, deny it or accept it and get on with his life. He realized he must accept the fact that in life there are no guarantees, that in spite of this uncertainty and the accompanying anxiety, he would still have to go on living, making choices and living responsibly with the consequences of his decisions. James chose to commit himself to therapy and discover himself what he might.

Mary's role was to gently guide James to look at his life. By providing a sounding board or mirror, Mary was to help James enlarge the range of his living. Through the process of becoming aware of and getting in touch with his past, James was able to begin to make new decisions and to accept responsibility for changing the patterns which affected his future.

During the first months of James' therapy, he felt depressed most of the time and often expressed a wish to die so that he wouldn't feel the helpless, emptiness and loneliness which drained his energy. He said he had nothing to look forward to, no purpose--only a past filled with mistakes and regrets. He said he had loved his son and when his son had died a big part of himself also had died.

Mary's goal was to provide adequate support for James. He needed an opportunity to talk about his regrets and what it felt like to be depressed. He needed to feel that he was being heard and that someone cared enough to listen. Meanwhile, without James realizing Mary challenged him to create a new meaning for life. He was encouraged to recount events in his past that he regretted and wished had been different. He was urged to talk about his son being gone and the loss of companionship he felt.

Mary did not ignore or play down James' depression, for in this symptom was a hidden message, as well as, a path to discovery. By beginning with James' own full recognition and acceptance of his feeling of hopelessness, Mary began guiding him to heal himself. She did not dwell extensively on these negative feelings either, and was especially interested in how James derived meaning through work and in what ways work contributed to his feeling that he had something to offer people. James was lead to discover that the relationship he had with his son was not the simple father/son bond as James had thought, that in not having had much of an adolescence of his own, he tried to make up for this gap in his youth through companionship with his son. Mary and James focused on the feelings he had for adolescents and what he learned from them. He admitted that he derived a great deal of personal pleasure from seeing young people search for meaning in their lives.

Although James needed this opportunity to relive times from the past, there was a danger that he would stop there, rather than getting on with his life in other, new directions. Mary was astute enough to know that James had, while alone and in piecemeal fashion, reviewed much of what they talked about together. She was aware that what she supplied was a means whereby James could integrate his total life experience, both the negative and positive aspects, in an open, caring atmosphere. James was no longer alone, but the decisions and subsequent actions still remained the responsibility of James.

At this point Mary was herself fearful of getting lost in the depression. If James did not find new hope and a will to continue to live, Mary could be threatened in many ways.

She might see that she could be faced with the same search for hope. If James did not move beyond depression, she could evaluate herself in terms of not having given enough to James, i.e. would James have found more meaning for living, if she was more of a person or more skilled in helping him at this juncture in his life?

So much depended on James and what he was willing to choose to do for himself. Mary could not allow herself to be duped into thinking that she could create a will to live for James, that she could do his healing for him, or that she would have, tailor-made answers. Within the existential model, which Mary had chosen to abide by in working with James, there was no 'professional distance'. The expert/client relationship of many of the other models was absent from the beginning and where James' therapy lead would largely be determined by his own willingness to begin to move himself by taking the initial steps. The best Mary could offer was the inspiration to begin taking those steps, the emotional support which could instill new hope and confidence in James. Through this relationship, James had the opportunity to see that he could move further than he previously allowed himself to imagine. Mary provided a spark of self-confidence and self-understanding which was the start of reversing his feelings of low self-esteem.

Cultural Factors

During the course of therapy, James felt comfortable in sharing his feelings about his Indian background and the cultural conflicts he experienced. He expressed some concern as to whether he would be able to integrate his Indian heritage with his life in a large western city. He discussed his religious beliefs and the importance they played in his life.

The philosophy of the Yakui elders has been one that aims to keep equilibrium between man and the spirits. According to the elders, everything in the world, animate and inanimate, plays a part in the religion and each is important in its relationship to the other. This belief teaches that the world is controlled by certain spiritual rules, and that man is assured a peaceful, long life only if he learns the rules and abides by them. By doing this he is sure of his harmony with the spirits. He is concerned with securing harmony in human, natural and supernatural relationships.

Success for James rests more in being a good person than in acquiring material things. If he collects too many material things he could be thought of as being selfish or stingy.

A Navajo wife accepts the husband as the formal head, but the wife, with her matrilineal descent, has as much, or more, influence in family management as does her husband.. The tangible necessities of life remain with the wife's extended family group. Her brothers contribute greatly to the teaching and discipline of the children. The Navajos do not speak of the deceased.

If the Navajo family moves from the reservation to an urban area, the following effects are apt to occur:

1. The woman is deprived of the company and support of the other members of her family.
2. The woman assumes total responsibility for care of her children, which was formerly shared with the grandmother, her sisters and aunts.
3. The woman no longer has easy access to the advice of the elders, her brothers, and others, in child-rearing and discipline.

Conflict has arisen for the Navajo woman as her role has been altered in three important ways:

1. Her function within the family as parent has greatly increased.
2. Her economic position has been undermined.
3. Her security and bargaining power in family interactions has been greatly reduced.

This conflict in the role of the Navajo woman and her beliefs had an adverse effect on James when he became unemployed and in grief. He felt more of a failure than he would have, had he continued to live on the reservation where he could have relied on his wife's farm and her extended family resources. He subsequently left his family.

Mary encouraged James to become involved with other Indian people living in his urban area as a means of developing a support system to function in place of his extended family. She also shared ideas with regard to embracing the best of both cultures, leaving the decision up to him as to what constituted 'the best'--the process of making those decisions served to help James integrate his past and present. In addition, she assured him that being laid off from his job had nothing to do with his masculinity or his competence as a provider; rather, it was only an example that life is at times unfair and unjust. She encouraged him to relate with other Indian men who had solved problems similar to his.

Mary, by displaying a sensitivity to cultural factors, was able to intervene and help James to act and to accept both the freedom of, and the responsibility for, his actions. James had become aware of those factors that limited his existence. He understood them to be a combination of external pressures and internal reactions. The critical aspect of James' therapy was his recognition that he had choices to make.

Mary explored with James the possibility of a reconciliation with his family since he was highly devoted and had left them when he felt he was a failure. He was open to relationship counseling and Mary was able to assist this family in reconciling and as a family work through their grief. Eventually this family returned to the reservation where appropriate spiritual ceremonies for the family of the deceased aided in the grief resolution and in the healing process for the survivors.

REFERENCES

English, H.B., & English, A.C. (1958). A COMPREHENSIVE DICTIONARY OF PSYCHOLOGICAL AND PSYCHOANALYTICAL TERMS: A GUIDE TO USAGE. New York: David McKay Co.

Kluckhohn, F.R. & Stodbeck, F.L. (1961). VARIATIONS IN VALUE ORIENTATIONS. New York: Harper & Row.

Nobles, W.W. (1979). The right of culture: a declaration for the provision of culturally sensitive mental health services and the issue of protected status. In MULTI-CULTURAL ISSUES OF MENTAL HEALTH SERVICES. California: Department of Mental Health, pp. 139-140.

Norton, Delores (1978). DUAL PERSPECTIVE, Council on Social Work Education. New York.

5. TOWARDS A HOLISTIC MODEL OF INTERVENTION

In reviewing the cultural values of American Indian populations and the importance of spirituality across all tribes, a modality which incorporates mind, body and spirit is important.

A holistic psychology is needed which incorporates the mind, body and spirit, to alleviate the sense of fragmentation which permeates our society today. In addition it is recognized that a psychology circumscribed by pathology can not lead to constructively dynamic social experiences. Psychoanalysis is neither an appropriate nor an adequate tool for the study of the cultural or historical dimensions of personality. Since the psyche has both a depth dimension and a time dimension (inwardly experienced) a holistic psychology seems most appropriate for greater understanding of these aspects of the personality.

A holistic approach then combines the spiritual, social, psychological and physical aspect of each person. The symbols and other processes of the unconscious then provide the psychological foundation for a society. In summary a holistic model of growth and health views the biological (physical) elements as less important than the historical and spiritual elements of humanity. A reductive and analytical view of humanity is replaced by one which synthesizes psychic (spiritual) content and recognizes the purposive nature of humanity. This involves a shift from a rationalistic view of life to an outlook that encompasses a larger conception of reality.

Since many American Indians believe in visions, rely on dreams as guidance from the spirit and experience what is considered paranormal phenomena on a regular basis, a different reality evolves. This reality has at its foundation a variety of spiritual values and beliefs.

Holistic Model

A holistic approach draws heavily from philosophy, social theory and the study of cultures. It is an open-ended model which is continually being revised as new truths are uncovered.

An <u>INNER PURPOSE</u> manifested through the personality is an extremely important element in this model's view of reality. Holism comes from an integration of the spiritual aspects with the physical and psychological aspects of the individual's personality. The spiritual elements of life are facts not illusions and are to be penetrated and lived on a daily basis.

In an effort to grasp a larger view of reality this model builds on the ancient religions and philosophies of American Indians and others and translates their thinking about psychic processes into terms that fit into a western orientation.

There is a great need for an understanding of the <u>Unconscious</u> which allows the dimensions of psychic reality available to people, without limiting them to group consensus for analysis and interpretation. A basic assumption of this model is that life requires the individual to confront the world on a cosmic and social level after looking within to find ones own essential purpose for life. This is an ongoing process as the individual struggles to find the light within. This process is enacted for example in the ritual of the vision quest of the Plains Indians when the young person passes from childhood into adulthood. This model holds that REALITY is revealed to us through scientific experimentation, intellectual analysis, creation of art, literature and music as well as altered states of consciousness. (Our mind acts as a machine which projects diverse images on the screen of life). The source of these images as well as symbols which come to us in dreams and fantasies remains a mystery. Theorists such as Jung referred to this source as the collective unconscious. American Indians attribute this knowledge to the Great Spirit's guidance. We can assume that the same images and forms which drive people to insanity can also be the source of our most creative inspirations.

Natural Healing Levels

Each individual has within their constitution a natural healing system which can be mediated internally or externally. The counselor can be a catalyst in setting in motion this healing process. Four levels of integration can be observed. These four levels are the physiological, the psychological, the social and the cultural meaning level of integration. A person who has experienced trauma can be comforted by a warm embrace by a significant other, they can be told that they are not to blame for the traumatic event to alleviate the psychological guilt which sometimes accompanies trauma. In addition the clients favorite foods may be prepared as a symbol of love and respect. Cultural healing ceremonies can be conducted for the benefit of the client. All of these activities are major contributors to the natural healing process of the client.

Because Indian people have been traumatized as a people for many years, the post traumatic stress can be intergenerational. Group acknowledgement of this oppression and healing rituals can be of great benefit in setting in motion the natural healing for large groups and communities.

Case Vignette: Mary, a thirty five year old Lakota woman began having nightmares about a Catholic priest who had been her high school teacher in a mission boarding school. The trauma of her rape and memories of the ongoing abuse for several years had been repressed for many years. The repressed memories were brought to the surface while watching a film on sexual abuse in a college classroom. Mary sought therapy for the post traumatic stress symptoms from a local Indian agency. She was seen individually for several sessions before collateral visits with her husband proved to be of major importance. He was educated about the psychological effects of sexual abuse and provided Mary with emotional support and understanding. He was encouraged to participate in surrounding Mary with a loving environment which included her favorite cultural foods, and inclusion in all social activities of the family. Mary sought assistance from a spiritual leader in the community and began attending sweat lodge ceremonies on a regular basis. The healing integration was observed on all four levels as Mary began to redefine herself as a person, not as damaged goods but as a restored, healed, wife and mother. Her self esteem was restored, she regained her self confidence lost in her youth and became a leader in her community. Interventions limited to the psychological level would not have been as effective in restoring the total functioning of this woman at the physiological, social and cultural levels of her awareness.

Native Americans like other people are influenced by the behavior of others toward them. Their family and friends along with their tribal affiliation shape their behavior, attitudes, values, self image and world view.

Attempts to alleviate suffering are usually labeled treatment and every society usually trains some of its members to assume this responsibility. Certain types of therapy rely upon the healers ability to mobilize healing forces within the client by psychological means. In the Native American community this responsibility is shared by spiritual leaders, medicine men and mental health counselors.

Mental Health Counseling

Since many forms of personal interaction may affect a person's sense of well-being and could be considered therapeutic, the definition of mental health counseling must of necessity be somewhat arbitrary. We shall consider as mental health counseling only the following:

1. A trained, socially sanctioned healer, whose healing powers are accepted by the sufferer and by his social or ethnic group.
2. A sufferer who seeks relief from a healer.
3. A series of contacts between the healer and the sufferer, through which the healer often with the aid of a group tries to produce certain changes in the sufferers emotional state, attitudes and behavior. (Frank, 1961).

Emotional Problems

   The words mentally ill and psychiatric treatment are not popular in the Native American community. Native American clients are more comfortable with the words counseling and emotional problems rather than the above.
   Native Americans, like other people, are subject to difficulty coping with their environment. A divorce, a death in the family or other crisis may create disturbances in thinking, feeling, and communicative behavior. Some clients may suffer from a distorted view of self, faulty communication with others or a damaging experience of early life.
   Mental health counseling cannot be divorced from cultural influences. Since Native Americans are primarily a spiritual people; healing rituals merge with mental health counseling to a great extent.
   Though spirituality is an important ingredient of Indian Counseling, one of the basic wishes of the traditional American Indian is that their spiritual attitudes, beliefs and ideologies not be discussed or examined. The Indian feels that to do so is to upset the balance and rightness of his/her cosmos. Thus, there are many limitations and restrictions upon what can be shared with non-Indians in the form of lectures and published articles. It is with this in mind that the focus of this section be concentrated on other aspects of Indian psychology.
   The "Indian philosophy" has recently come into sharp focus--as more and more Americans become disenchanted with the emptiness of materialism. In addition national concern about ecology has turned the attention of the masses toward the native peoples who for untold centuries lived in harmony with man, animals and nature.

The Indian Gestalt View

   The average Indian knows one's mind intimately. Some believe that they are born with natural abilities to look into the future as well as communicate non-verbally with other people. Present day researchers in parapsychology have agreed that American Indians possess psychic abilities far surpassing all other ethnic groups. The Indian sees the mind, body and spirit as inseparable. Feelings are the most important unit of human function giving meaning to life. The gestalt form of perception, which seems intuitive among Indians is in sharp contrast to the preoccupation of Anglo-American psychologists with analysis of personality variables to the 4th decimal point.

"The non-verbalized communication of Indians is described best by DeLoria.

Most meetings held by Indians come to no conclusion which could be understood as agreements to do certain things. But every person attending a high-level meeting of Indians knows exactly what course of action will be supported by the majority of tribes and exactly how to interpret the actions of the meeting to his people" (DeLoria, 1970).

Indians as a general rule do not relate to the descriptions and dynamics of abnormal psychology or ego psychology. They wish to emphasize feelings. The capacity to "feel" is experienced in terms of "Vibrations" received from other Indians and understood by them. This allows automatic communication by non-verbal means. It is clear then that the striving for precise verbality among whites is foreign to the American Indian's concept of communication.

Understatement and trance continue to be a basic part of the Indian style of Counseling.

It is interesting to note that the seventeenth-century Iroquois, as described in detail by Jesuit missionaries, actually practiced a dream analysis which was remarkably similar to Freud's discovery two hundred years later in Vienna (Farb, 1968). The Iroquois tribe recognized the existence of an unconscious, the force of unconscious desires, how the conscious mind attempts to repress unpleasant thoughts, how these unpleasant thoughts emerge in dreams and how the frustration of unconscious desires may cause mental and physical (psychosomatic) illnesses. The Iroquois faith in dreams is only somewhat diminished after more than three hundred years.

Indian Counseling may take the form of relaxed story telling with the use of indirect suggestion and metaphor frequently appearing in the legends. Because of the low economic status of many American Indians it is no surprise that emotional strain is evident. Counseling must of necessity focus on alleviation of environmental pressures related to housing, food and medical care.

The Assumptive World of American Indians

Each person develops assumptions about himself and the world in which he lives based upon his experiences, enabling him to predict the behavior of others and the outcome of his own actions. The totality of each persons assumptions may be called his "assumptive world". The assumptive world of the American Indian reflects a distrust of societal institutions based upon negative experiences with the federal government and other institutions. Included is a distaste for the educational process which forbade the cultural practices of religion, Native language and the art of beading. Because the assumptive world is the sum total of attitudes based on experiences either negative or positive it is important to discuss the process related to the formulation of attitudes involving the emotional state accompanying the initial experience. Attitudes that are connected with a sense of uncertainty or confusion or with the prediction of an unfavorable outcome tend to generate unpleasant emotions such as anxiety, panic and despair. Those that give a person a sense of security and promise a better future are related to feelings of hope, faith and security. These emotional states largely determine a person's state of well-being.

Attitudes may be enduring or transient. Some attitudes are held with firm conviction and endure from one generation to another. One such attitude is the American Indian's distrust of the federal government based upon the long history of oppression and control of the land, their health and their education. It is no wonder that American Indian's have difficulty relating to white mental health personnel regardless of how good the intentions. The white therapist in most instances is at a great disadvantage because of the assumptive world of the American Indian client. On the other hand an American Indian therapist has a great advantage because of the client's assumption that the therapist can be trusted. The American Indian therapist can engender feelings of faith, hope and security without even trying.

Cultural Conflict

Many Indian people suffer from an identity crisis brought on by the clash of their tribal culture and the American white middle class culture.

The values of individualism, future orientation, competitiveness, materialism and strong self importance are in conflict with Indian values which are directly opposite.

The following chart includes other conflicting values which are a source of confusion and frustration to Indian clients. It is important to note that many well meaning therapists impose Anglo values on Indian clients as a result of their ignorance of Indian values.

INDIANNESS
AMERICAN INDIAN IDENTITY CONTINUUM
Degree of Indian Blood

ASSIMILATED AMERICAN		INDIAN
Urban/Industrial values		Tribal/Traditional values
individual emphasis	---------- ----------	group, clan emphasis
future oriented	---------- ----------	present oriented
time, awareness	---------- ----------	time, non-awareness
youth	---------- ----------	age
competition, concern	---------- ----------	cooperation, service
conquest of nature	---------- ----------	concern for groups
saving	---------- ----------	harmony with nature
theoretical	---------- ----------	giving
impatience	---------- ----------	pragmatic
skeptical	---------- ----------	patience
guilt	---------- ----------	mystical
social coercion	---------- ----------	shame
immediate family	---------- ----------	permissiveness
materialistic	---------- ----------	extended family, clan
aggressive	---------- ----------	non-materialistic
overstates, over-confident	---------- ----------	non-aggressive
noise	---------- ----------	modest
converts others to religion	---------- ----------	silence
religion - segment of life	---------- ----------	respects other religion
land, water, forest		land, water, forest
private domain	---------- ----------	belongs to all
avarice and greedy		beneficial, reasonable
use of resources	---------- ----------	use of resources
wealth	---------- ----------	equality
representative gov't.	---------- ----------	face to face gov't.
space living, privacy,		compact living, close
use of roominess	---------- ----------	contact, indoors high
		space utilization
strong self importance	---------- ----------	low self value

_____DECULTURATION TREND_____
_____ACCULTURATION TREND_____

Choice of Modality

The modality most appropriate in counseling American Indians (where many tribes are represented such as an urban Indian center) is Carl Rogers' non-directive client centered approach. American Indians are uncomfortable with a direct probing approach and will usually withdraw and become non-communicative. A non-direct visiting approach will bring much better results in gaining information for an initial assessment.

The exception here is in cases of extreme crisis. In this instance a more direct approach is tolerated because the client is suffering extreme mental anguish and is desperate for any counselor to alleviate the suffering.

Modalities of cojoint family therapy and conjoint marriage counseling are appropriate when adapted to the tribal culture. Gestalt techniques are usually inappropriate as Native Americans are hesitant to play roles and participate in exercises of fantasy. Transactional Analysis has been used by some counselors in alcoholic programs with some success. The existential and phenomenological theoretical approach are in harmony with much of Native American religion and philosophy. The Gestalt philosophy of wholeness is appropriate, it is the techniques for achieving this which are inappropriate.

Treatment of Psychotic Clients

Psychotic clients are accepted by the American Indian community and there is no visible evidence to ostracize them from social activities. This attitude is in harmony with the denial of mental illness as such and the reluctance to consider emotional problems as mental illness.

Many urban Indian Centers function as community mental health centers with social groups that include the socially isolated (psychotic clients) such as youth groups, women's groups and other activities. Mental health services are delivered in these agencies by American Indian social workers who are educated to work with clients suffering from depression, schizophrenia, family problems and family crises. These services have arisen in response to the emerging needs of American Indians adjusting to environmental pressures of the urban community.

Social Group Work with American Indians

When groups are used in social work practice, labels such as group therapy, group treatment and focus groups are applied. When social work is practiced with people in groups, the elements of the configuration include a collection of people participating with each other and with a facilitator to achieve mutual goals.

American Indian group work in order to be effective must be based on common cultural values of cooperation rather than competition and conflict. The Talking Circle, a spiritual healing ceremony has been adapted by many agencies to achieve many of the objectives of group work. Usually the facilitator is of American Indian heritage, but adapted forms of the circle may not require this. The participants in the group form a circle with the facilitator or leader beginning by explaining the rules. No one must leave the group until everyone has had an opportunity to speak. No one is required to speak if they choose not to. Usually the leader opens with a prayer to the Great Spirit and then turns to the person their left and invites them to share with the group anything they feel led to share. Other group members do not comment or disagree with what is said. After each member of the group speaks the person on their left is given the opportunity. Participants may sing a song, offer a prayer for individuals, for the group or the community, or speak from their own concerns and/or problems. After everyone has had an opportunity to speak the leader closes with prayer and the group adjourns.

Other types of groups that have proven effective with American Indian participants are dream groups, where participants share dreams and discuss their meaning. This type of group can be led by a mental health professional or a lay person from the Indian community.

Women support groups focusing on parenting, weight control, stress management, and other topics of interest are also popular in Indian agencies. Activity groups which promote Indian art, beading, pottery, poetry, creative writing and other activities have also been effective in promoting individual growth and development.

Other groups for recovery from substance abuse includes communication skill development, healthy lifestyle promotion, codependency, anger, and assertiveness as a focus. Many Alcoholic Anonymous groups are conducted with a cultural approach unique to the tribal group.

Family Therapy with American Indians

Family therapy with American Indians is conducted in the family home in most instances in order to include extended family members living with the nuclear family. This usually includes a grandparent, aunts, uncles or cousins.

Grandparents in many instances are assuming a strong leadership role in these families and serve as a stabilizing force for many single parents. The input from the grandparent is of utmost importance in the psychosocial assessment of the family dynamics. This grandparent or other elder in the home is a key focus of the intervention, as very little progress will take place without their support. The family therapist must move slowly and listen intently before attempting any major interventions with the family. Usually the changes must be interpreted for the family as in harmony with their basic view of the function of the family. Family ties are very strong with the group having a great amount of influence on younger members, especially young single parents. To encourage the single parent to become an individualist and move into their own apartment may be seen as divisive to the rest of the family. This would be grounds for terminating therapy in some instances.

In the Lakota tribes in South Dakota, the oldest grandchild is often reared by the grandparents from infancy. This is based upon tradition and not on any particular favoritism over other grandchildren. These children usually become very responsible adults with much respect for the elders in the community.

The pace of therapy is usually slow, with the family taking the lead. A non-directive visiting approach is most appropriate with care not to interrupt until a family member is finished making their point. The facilitator should be prepared for long periods of silence and strive to avoid probing for answers. Usually the more the therapist probes the more the family resists sharing information until they deem the time is appropriate. Gestalt techniques of talking to chairs is not appropriate with most strongly identified American Indians. It is important for the therapist to know the tribal expectations of men and women in a particular tribal group. If the man is to be the spokesperson for the family this should be acknowledged. In some instances it is more effective to have a team approach with both a male and female therapist working together. Many Indian men may be uncomfortable talking only to a female therapist. On the other hand many tribes have had special leadership roles for women and this should be acknowledged. It is wise for the therapist to become knowledgeable about the tribal background of the family and then assess what level of assimilation is present before proceeding with any type of psychotherapy.

Grief Counseling

As mental health programs for American Indians are developed, there is an increasing need for mental health practitioners to understand the burial customs among Indian tribes if services are to be therapeutic. It follows that any discussion of grief counseling must take into consideration the values of the Indian client, philosophy of life, attitude toward death, cultural traditions, and assumptive world (Kubler-Ross, 1969). This section will discuss the complexities of grief counseling in the Indian community, encompassing behavioral stereotypes, customs and counseling techniques. Before this discussion takes place we first need to follow the migration of Indian people from the reservations into urban areas.

Stereotypes

Tribal affiliation is the American Indian's most basic identification. The tribal teachings and experiences determine to a great extend the personality, values and life goals of the individual, including the meaning of death and customs surrounding the burial of the dead. Because of extreme forms of discrimination toward Indians in certain parts of the country, many Indians have denied their tribal affiliation in fear of losing their lives or suffering physical harm.

The attitude of American society towards American Indians is a strangely ambivalent one. The popular holistic health movement with its emphasis on the harmony of body, mind, and spirit embraces to a great extent the world view of American Indians with their emphasis on the natural harmony of all living things. American Indian art and jewelry have never been more popular. People everywhere seem to be wearing turquoise rings, bracelets, and necklaces handcrafted by Indian silversmiths. Indian symbols and designs are found on the wallpaper, bedspreads, and rugs of plush Fifth Avenue apartments. Indian-designed sweaters are seen from coast to coast. It would appear that Indian culture is to be admired and embraced.

On the other hand, social scientists, television, and the film industry portray a drunken Indian, suicidal and hopeless. American Indians are either to be glorified and idealized as having mystical wisdom or ridiculed and stigmatized as being the shame of society. Mental health practitioners need to understand the self-image predicament American Indians find themselves in when reacting to these extremely positive or negative stereotypes. The Indian client desires to be seen as a human being, with feelings of pride in ones heritage and a desire for others to respect ones beliefs and cultural traditions.

Negative stereotypes of American Indians contribute to false impressions of behavioral adjustment (Shore, 1974). One commonly held assumption is that Indians as a group have many psychiatric problems and there is no hope for them (Beiser, 1974). After working with American Indians of over a hundred tribes in the San Francisco Bay Area, the author recalls a dramatic example of a young Hopi man experiencing auditory hallucinations after a family death. The local psychiatric emergency ward erroneously interpreted the hallucination as a psychotic symptom rather than part of the symptom complex associated with unresolved grief. An Indian agency intervened and this man was returned to the reservation to participate in a series of rituals and tribal ceremonies appropriate for the burial of the dead. Shortly after the ceremony he was free from the hallucinations. This man could have been hospitalized in a state mental hospital as a psychotic patient if American Indian mental health personnel had not intervened on his behalf. In most instances practices that are difficult to understand are usually interpreted as indicators of psychopathology by the dominant society. There are other examples of a blending of healing and worship for the improvement of mental health as opposed to a diagnosis of pathology and long term treatment (Bergmen, 1973).

Burial Practices

Some urban Indians migrate back to the reservations when old age approaches. Many who have lived most of their adult lives in the city wish to be buried, when death comes, on their home reservation. This creates problems of a financial nature for the survivors, since to do so entails two funerals and additional costs to transport the deceased. Some tribal offices will give assistance in providing funds for travel for survivors and funeral costs depending on the amount of funds available. For some the desire to return to the homeland is indicative of a sacredness of the land. Some tribal cultures have been accustomed to having wakes for the family of the deceased. This is prevented in many urban areas as a violation of city and state laws. Thus the grieving process is sometimes interrupted and delayed until years later (Kubler-Ross, 1969). A few tribes have a specific number of days set aside for the mourner to grieve. During this time no work is done by the mourners. Friends of the family take care of the cooking and other necessary housekeeping chores. Other tribal beliefs require the deceased to be buried within 24 hours. This creates problems for the families in urban areas when funeral directors are insensitive to these beliefs and fail to cooperate.

The Language of Grief

Nothing can begin to compensate for the loss of a loved one. Similarly, words cannot fully express ones grief feelings. The loneliness, emptiness, and sadness cannot be adequately conveyed. Even the most eloquent C.S. Lewis wrote:
"Grief feels most like fear. No one ever told me loss felt like fear. The fluttering in my stomach, the same yawning, and I keep swallowing. Perhaps, more strictly, it feels like suspense. Or like waiting, just hanging about waiting for something to happen. I can't settle down. I fidget. I smoke too much. Up until this loss I had too little time. Now there is nothing but time."

(Lewis, 1961)

Colin Murray Parker saw grieving resembling a physical injury: "The loss may be spoken of as a blow. As in the case of a physical injury, the 'wound' heals gradually. But occasionally complications set in, healing is delayed, or a further injury reopens a healing wound" (Parker, 1972). Edgar N. Jackson wrote, "Grief is a universal human experience. It is the strong emotion we feel when we come face to face with the death of someone who has been a part of our lives" (Jackson, 1961). Emotions cannot truly be described. In attempting to express our grief, the deepest and truest things about our feelings will stay unsaid. Words grow fewer. Touching or being touched "says" more than words. Memories from childhood remind us that a touch is the most comforting mode of communication available to us.

Counseling Techniques

It is important in grief counseling to assess the meaning of death, the customs surrounding funerals and the personal wishes of the client survivor. The treatment of the deceased after death is of utmost importance as is the participation for some American Indians in tribal rituals and ceremonies. Interruptions in these processes have a direct effect on resolution of the grief process of the survivors (Bergman, 1973).

In counseling American Indian clients who are experiencing grief, the author has found Ira Tanner's method most effective (Tanner, 1976). His method includes information on the facts of healing, validation, and confrontation. The client needs to know what feelings to expect in order to allow the grieving process to flow naturally. Clients need to hear from others that the loss had indeed happened. Funerals and tribal ceremonies help to validate the reality of a death. Responsible and sensitive confrontation is sometimes necessary for sound physical and emotional healing. Knowledge of tribal beliefs is very important.

The client survivor should be encouraged to share feelings and ventilate anger. The bereaved may need help for months after the funeral to allow them to work through their feelings of guilt and anger (Kubler-Ross, 1969). It is important that the practitioner tolerate the client's anger, regardless of whether it is directed at the deceased, at God, or at the helping professions. In this way the bereaved takes a step toward acceptance of the loss without guilt. If we blame the client for feeling angry we may prolong their grief, shame, and guilt, often resulting in physical and emotional ill-health.

Because of the cultural and communication barriers existing between some American Indians and societal institutions it is sometimes necessary for the mental health practitioner to play an active role in the funeral arrangements and legal steps after a death. This may involve assistance with disposal of property, assistance with obtaining social security benefits, obtaining the death certificate, legal assistance, etc. Social workers frequently act as advocates for clients with funeral arrangements, especially when the deceased is transported back to the home reservation. For this reason the social work profession plays and integral part in grief counseling of American Indians.

When social workers and other mental health practitioners becomes aware of the cultural factors involved in the symptom complex associated with unresolved grief for American Indians, the incidence of grief resolution should occur more frequently with these clients.

REFERENCES

Beiser, M. (1974). Indian Mental Health. PSYCHIATRIC ANNALS, 4(9), 6-8.

Bergman, R.L. (1973). Navajo Medicine and Psychoanalysis. HUMAN BEHAVIOR, 2, 9-15.

DeLoria, Vine Jr. (1970). WE TALK YOU LISTEN, MacMillan Co., New York.

Farb, Peter (1968). MAN'S RISE TO CIVILIZATION, Avon Books.

Frank, Jerome (1961). PERSUASION AND HEALING, Schocken Books.

Jackson, E.J. (1961). YOU AND YOUR GRIEF, New York: Channel Press.

Kubler-Ross, E. (1969). DEATH AND DYING. New York: MacMillan Publishing Co.

Lewis, C.S. (1961). A GRIEF OBSERVED. New York: Seabury Press.

Parker, C.M. (1971). BEREAVEMENT, STUDIES OF GRIEF IN ADULT LIFE. New York: International Studies Press.

Shore, J.H. (1974). Psychiatric Epidemiology Among American Indians. PSYCHIATRIC ANNALS, 4(9), 56-64.

Tanner, I. (1976). THE GIFT OF GRIEF. New York: Hawthorn Books.

United States Department of Commerce (1970). Bureau of Census. Subject Report, American Indians. Washington, DC: Government Printing Office.

6. ISSUES OF AMERICAN INDIAN WOMEN

"With eyes tightly closed
ye must dance.
To you who dare to see
Forever red thine eyes
will be."

An Indian Song (La Pointe, 1976)

The New Indian Woman is dramatically moving from the safe protected environment of the home into the competitive arenas of politics, higher education and administration. This chapter, written from the perspective of a Lakota educator provides an overview of the internal and external forces acting upon the Indian woman today.

In the last decade Urban Indian women have become increasingly active in the political arena. The shortage of Indian men and other changing circumstances have created a demand for more active participation of Indian women in all phases of Indian life. On the other hand the active participation of Indian women in positions formerly held by men is seen as emasculation by many Indian men.

This activity on the part of Indian women has many consequences. Indian men (as other men) are sometimes resentful of being supervised by women administrators and are reluctant to serve on boards dominated by women. Indian women receive little support from the men in dealing with the added pressures of administrative responsibilities in additional to normal family demands. Additional stress is placed upon the Indian family as this trend continues.

From "The Urban Indian Woman and Her Family" by Wynne Hanson, Social Casework (October 1980). Vol. 62, No. 8, pp. 476-483. Copyright 1980, Family Service American. Reprinted by permission.

Historical Background

The American Indian woman today is influenced by internal and external forces which have their antecedents in tribal history, in historical events from before and after initial contact with the European culture.

Literature about Indian women living in the early 1700's, before contact with the white settlers, is sparse. Anthropological studies which exist are written from the perspective of the white male, in which "...Native women have been referred to as drudges, beasts of burden, and other demoralizing terms." (Medicine, 1977). It is more than possible that Indian women in history were not permitted to interact with non-Indian men due to cultural constraints. Margaret Mead conducted a careful study of the Indian woman's role (Mead, 1932). Her work is a most comprehensive guide to the student of the American Indian. Despite the deficiencies of anthropological studies to accurate portray the early American Indian women, it is still possible to gain enough information to recreate the status and role of the Indian woman and her activities in the pre-reservation tribal setting by referring to Indian writers such as La Point and Medicine.

> "you must endeavor to lead wholesome lives. Many bold young men with persuasive tongues will whisper convincing talk in your ear. They will hold you. You will be tempted. Restrain yourself; do not answer the call of nature. You will know when your man comes along. There will be pleasurable times for you. Teach your children to walk upon the red road (equivalent to the white man's straight and narrow path). Teach them to be mindful of the weak and the needy. Teach them to share their fortunes with others. Base emotions are harmful and must be repressed."
>
> A Formula for Proper Living Given
> to Young Indian Virgins
> (La Pointe, 1976)

It is impossible to describe the early life of women with the diversity of tribes. The Lakota tribe has been selected for the purpose of presenting the Indian woman as a unique and viable being who shares a body of common experience with all women of diverse cultures. The Lakota women were exceptionally vigorous, healthy and active women. The Lakota tribe viewed the woman as someone with a peaceful heart, someone who was kind and gentle. The Indian man regarded his wife most kindly, and the people remembered the woman's high place in the tribe.

When the woman consented to marriage she vowed to perform her work properly and act in a manner that honored her husband. Two or three days after the man's proposal for marriage she might present him a pair of moccasins to reveal her willingness to live as his wife. Her father and relatives, by keeping his gifts, made know their approval. Her new husband might brush and arrange her hair in the manner her father looked after her mother's hair.

It was the woman's role to rise at dawn and prepare food for her family. This meant carrying wood and water and building a fire. When these chores were completed she tidied up the lodge and relaxed to her quilling of moccasins for the family members. She tanned hides for robes and lodge covers to use when needed. Later, after the dinner was served and cleared away the family settled down for a long evening of story telling, teasing, and play. The Indian woman, independent for the post part, played a submissive supportive role to the husband. She could express her concerns, but he made most decisions affecting the family. It was also acceptable for the husband to take additional wives, sometimes younger sisters of his wife, if they were left widowed. They would assist in the homemaking chores of food preparation and tanning. This custom brought much sadness and mental anguish to some women as they competed for the husband's affection and attention. It was not uncommon for women to commit suicide by hanging when their husbands took a second, younger wife!

By the early 1800's, the white fur traders began to trade guns, beads and alcohol to the Lakota Indians in exchange for furs. It was at this time that a breakdown of the cultural customs began. Indian men and women under the influence of alcohol began to neglect their families and tribal responsibilities. Indian women began to inter-marry with the English and French fur traders. In 1805, the United States government coerced tribal leaders into signing treaties they could not read thus not understand (Costo, 1977). By 1862, these treaties opened the territory to homesteaders and miners who flocked in by the hundreds and thousands. Almost immediately after contact with the Europeans, Indians began to suffer a decline in health. By the middle 1800's epidemics of cholera, measles and smallpox wiped out entire villages.

> "Where my people fall and now lie buried,
>   those lands are still mine..."
>
> Crazy Horse

Soon after, the Indian families were forced to adapt to life on the reservation. This adaptation slowly destroyed a way of life that had been functional for thousands of years. The Sacred Black Hills were taken by an illegal treaty, the buffalo were destroyed for furs, and the language and religious practices were forbidden by the missionary schools. Children were torn from their parents to begin the long process of assimilation (or genocide).

In 1849, the Bureau of Indian Affairs was given full authority to oversee the activities of Indian people.

In 1877, the land was divided into allotments and individual ownership was given to Indians who were to become farmers and ranchers, (Dawes Act). The Indian men who had lived by hunting buffalo and deer now had to find new fields of achievement. There was no opportunity for recognition as a brave warrior or a great hunter. He did not even have the joy of watching his children grow to adulthood. They were strangers to him if and when they returned from the missionary boarding schools (Merian, 1928). The Indian women suffered as well. She quietly watched her children taken from her and painfully saw the deterioration of her husband as dreams of self fulfillment became less and less of a reality (Coolidge, 1977).

In the middle of the 1900's Congress passed the Relocation Act of 1952 (Stuart, 1977). The Bureau of Indian Affairs hoped to assimilate the Indians into the mainstream of the population by encouraging them to move to the cities with promises of training and jobs. The Indians like other ethnic migrants formed their own communities in the cities for emotional support and survival. From 1952 through 1968 some 67,522 Indians (heads of households) were relocated through this direct employment program.

Today there are more Indians living in urban areas than on the reservations (US Census, 1990).

Most Indian families adjusted to urban life at great emotional and spiritual cost. Others could not adjust and eventually returned to the reservation even more discouraged than before. The Urban Indian Centers evolved out of this need for fellowship, emotional support and a sense of community. During the last twenty years, Urban Indian Centers have been the prime providers of social services to Indians mainly because of Indian staffing and relevant casework services (Ablon, 1971). The personnel staffing Urban Indian Centers, themselves relocatees, provide a warm friendly welcome to newly arrived Indians and provide social activities to assist them in the adjustment process.

The number of contemporary studies of Indian women are few, except for Gridley's NATIVE AMERICAN WOMEN (1974) which addresses the adjustment of Indian women in boarding schools, her alienation from family and lack of employment opportunities on the reservation. A more recent contemporary study was conducted by Bea Medicine, a Lakota Anthropologist, THE NATIVE AMERICAN WOMAN (1978).

A lucidly written study from an anthropological perspective is most rewarding to read. It is essential for anyone teaching or working with Indian women.

There is a great need for literature which portrays the Indian woman of today. What are her aspirations, her goals, her conflicts and her successes? It is important to the Indian Community to be aware of where women are going and what impact they have in the areas of education, law, human services, health, politics, employment and family life.

The aspirations of Indian women are to somehow combine the best of two worlds, to survive and to keep their families intact. To achieve these goals requires many Indian women to enter the world of the employed. The necessity of employment creates conflicts in dividing loyalties between family and career. The responsibility for teaching the cultural traditions to the young usually falls on the Indian woman. Indian operated day care centers help to alleviate this problem as the Indian culture is usually emphasized in the instruction of the children.

A philosophy which still persists is faith in a spirit world which Indian women turn to for guidance and strength. The extended family for some women provides a natural support system in times of crisis. Other women choose to request assistance from Urban Indian Centers or Community Mental Health Centers.

Residual persistences with roots in the tribal culture can be observed in the personalities of most Indian women.

Residual Persistences

Many tribal characteristics have survived and persisted in spite of strong external pressures to assimilate. The oral tradition of passing information from one generation to the next has persisted and is a commonality of all tribes. Spiritual values, generosity, autonomy and decisions by consensus have also persisted in most tribes. The harmony of all living things, and reverence for the land underlie the basic philosophy of most Indian people. Many mannerisms which are uniquely tribal have also persisted. The Lakota mannerism of pointing with ones chin is one of many which could be noted.

A modern thesis, put forward with some empirical findings, proposes a correlation between basic personality structure and cultural persistence. Irving Hallowell conducted a study to determine the degree of agreement or conformity existing between the observable acculturated behavior and the covert, inner life of the people (1925). The outline of post-contact Chippewa culture was reconstructed based upon accounts of explorers, fur traders, missionaries and others who had close association with the Indians in the Seventeenth and Eighteenth centuries. This material was supplemented by field observations and projective tests administered to adults and children.

He found "a considerable body of evidence that points to a persistent core of psychological characteristics sufficient to identify a tribal personality constellation, that is clearly discernible through all levels of acculturation yet studied."

There may be disagreement in naming the elements that should be included in such a psychological inventory. Some commonalities are the following: restrained and non-demonstrative emotional bearings, high degree of control over aggressive acts, acceptance of pain, hardship, hunger and frustration without voicing complaint, dependence upon supernatural power, and joking relationships with kinsmen as a device for relieving pressure within the group.

Other residual persistences can be observed which allow Indian women to maintain unique manifestations of tribalness. It was a custom for Lakota women to instruct their daughters and granddaughters in proper conduct through adulthood. On the other hand sons were turned over to the father at age ten for instruction and guidance and rarely had direction from their mothers thereafter. Evidence of these practices can still be observed in Lakota families. Unfortunately in fatherless homes the young sons are without guidance and mothers are reluctant to assume this responsibility. This manifestation of tribalness is an example of residual persistence. The values, belief systems and parenting practices of the tribe determine the status and role of women within each culture. Indian women also respond to internal and external forces within a context that is acceptable to their tribal affiliation. No to do so creates internal conflict. When residual persistence is minimal Indian women experience less internal conflict and role strain.

Internal and external forces acting on American Indian women today elicit varying responses. Inherent in the response to these social forces is the psychological set and the cultural value configuration of tribal affiliation and the degree of assimilation into the ambient society.

The Emerging Personality

The psychological set for Indian women as well as others is dependent upon historical events, genetic influences and their psycho-social development. Culture determines some personality traits and assigns the roles as well as the expectations. For most Indian women (as well as non-Indian women) the role is subservient to the male role. Hers has been primarily the role of homemaker. The <u>new</u> Indian woman is experiencing role transition.

The Indian woman depends upon her tribal affiliation for her basic identity and self image. Because of extreme forms of discrimination toward Indians in some parts of the country, many Indians have denied their tribal affiliation in fear of suffering physical harm. The result is that some Indian women suffer from this need to hide their identity. Other factors which contribute to a negative self image are media stereotypes which portray Indians as cruel savages or drunken and hopeless. In many instances practices that are difficult to understand are usually interpreted as indicators of psychopathology by the dominant society. Many practices of Indian people are misunderstood and diagnosed pathological.

Indian women have accepted some of the customs of the dominant society in the process of assimilation. Some assimilated Indian women prefer professional counselors when they are in need of guidance rather than turning to extended family or traditional healers.

Indian administrators find decisions by consensus are unworkable in large social agencies with federal and state accountability.

It appears that the assimilated Indian woman with minimal residual persistences experiences less internal conflict and role strain.

Case Vignettes

The following case vignettes provide a glimpse of Indian women who successfully face new challenges in a changing world. Living in a pluralistic society, they maintain their unique manifestations of tribalness. They are aware of having lost something of great value never to be replaced in the new world in which they live. They are, however, faithful guardians of what can be preserved of their cultural traditions and values. Chosen are five women who were reared on the reservation and migrated to the urban area in search of a better life. They are healthy, motivated women who successfully made the transition from reservation life to urban life. Their age range is 35 to 65. All attending boarding schools at sometime in their life. Each married an Indian man. They represent different tribes and educational levels. The tribes represented are Blackfeet, Lakota, Chippewa and Creek. These women did not have the support of an extended family in their successful adjustment to urban life. The names and historical events of their lives have been changed to disguise their identity. They presently live in several states.

Delphine is a 63 year old Lakota woman, married mother of four grown children. She was the third of ten children born to Lakota parents. Her mother was orphaned at age 9 and spent most of her life in boarding schools. The mother graduated from Carlyle Indian School at age 21. She never smoked, drank or wore make up. She was a devoted mother who never worked outside of the home. She was converted to Catholicism in boarding school, and reared her 9 surviving children in the church. Her guiding rule which she lived by was, "the womens' place is in the home". Delphine's father dropped out of school in 4th grade. He married Delpine's mother at age 30. Most of his adult life was spent farming and raising herefords on a 2000 acre ranch. Delphine's parents remained married until death and lived on the same ranch for 43 years.

Delphine attending boarding school and upon graduation from high school attended Haskel Institute in Lawrence, Kansas, where she majored in business. After graduation she met and married a Lakota man and moved to Minneapolis. The marriage ceremony was performed by a Lakota medicine man. Delphine and her husband were both in their late twenties at the time of their marriage. For several years Delphine chose to work before having children. The couple purchased a home in a quiet residential neighborhood. After the birth of their first child Delphine quit her job and assumed the role of full-time homemaker. She became active on school committees and was a devoted mother to their three daughters and one son. When the youngest child started school, Delphine returned to work as a secretary for the school district. Her job allowed her to work while the children were in school and to spend the summers at home. During the child rearing years the family returned several times a year to the reservation to visit family and friends and to participate in religious ceremonies. Their co-workers in the city became their support system.

This was a close knit family with Delphine internalizing her mother's emphasis on homemaking. Delphine experienced little role conflict in arranging to work when the children were in school. She still was able to use her business training to pursue her personal goals. Delphine has continuously honored the male personality of her Lakota husband by remaining submissive to his leadership in the home, and in the rearing of their son. The couple purchased a twenty acre parcel of land and built a small retirement cabin. It was their dream to return to the country after retirement. They appear to be content in this heavily wooded area that borders a private lake in Wisconsin. Their four children and their families are frequent visitors and Delphine and her husband enjoy teaching the Lakota history to their grandchildren.

Mary is a 46 year old Lakota woman who was orphaned at age 13, and reared by an older sister. She was the youngest of 5 children. She married a Lakota man at age 18. They moved to an urban area in search of a better life. Mary gave birth to 3 children during 15 years of marriage. The accidental death of her husband ended her marriage. As a young widow with children to rear she turned to personnel at the local Urban Indian Center as a support system. She accepted AFDC until she completed nurses training. After graduation she accepted employment in private nursing for several years. Then she became interested in psychology. She is now completing work on her Masters degree in psychology. Mary works as an administrator in a social service agency. She has supervised male social workers from her own tribe as well as the Southwest tribes. She has sensed a resentment on their part in responding to a woman supervisor. Mary has been very active on community boards. She experiences little conflict in asserting herself as a community leader. She did not assume an active role, however, until she became widowed. Her education has also contributed to her leadership skills along with external forces encouraging her to speak out for her clients.

Mary experiences some role conflict between career and motherhood. Being single she must be the solitary parent to three children living at home. She frequently attends Pow Wows and spends much of her off-duty hours with her children and grandchildren. She is a remarkably strong woman. Mary arises at 5 a.m. to complete homemaking chores before going to work. She frequently attends classes which last until late evening. Her children have been trained to prepare meals and function in her absence. They are also taught to think and make decisions independently which is a Lakota tradition.

Justine is a 52 year old Chippewa woman. She is married and the mother of 2 children. She attended boarding school and two years of Junior College. She relocated to the urban area under the Relocation Act. During her first years in the city, she worked as a Nurses Aid until she entered a human service training program at the Junior College level. Since then she has worked as a social worker and more recently as an agency director. She is an energetic woman with an optimistic attitude. She has been active on many boards and in community activities. She attends local Pow Wows and cultural activities with enthusiasm. She has experienced some resentment from Indian men working under her supervision. She has handled these incidents tactfully.

Justine has an unhappy marriage and is presently separated from her husband. She has experienced the problem of holding a more prestigious and higher paying job than her husband which has contributed to their marital problems. She has, however, a strong sense of purpose in helping Indian people which appears to be more gratifying to her than her marriage relationship. Her 2 children are college students with majors in human services. She does not acknowledge any role strain between career and motherhood. She has a positive relationship with her children.

Juanita is a 55 year old Blackfeet woman, married with no children. Her husband, a Chippewa, is a retired carpenter who spends most of his time doing volunteer work with the Indian elderly. Juanita has worked for 25 years as a bookkeeper in an Indians Arts and Crafts Center. Their support system has been personnel from the local Urban Indian Center. Juanita has held a homemaker role combined with an office career. This couple attends all Pow Wows and Indian cultural affairs. Trips to their reservation in Red Lake, Minnesota have been taken on an annual basis. In this way ties are maintained with relatives and friends. They have spent 25 years in the urban area and are undecided where they will live their retirement. They have been active in Indian bowling and athletic leagues over the years. The leagues have also served as a support system.

Kathy is a 35 year old Creek, mother of three children, married to a Choctaw man. She was raised in a foster home before moving to the urban area. Kathy worked as a bookkeeper before attending college, where she majored in social work. After graduating with a BA, she was accepted into law school. Kathy separated from her husband and later became active in the American Indian Movement. Kathy sees herself as a leader in the Indian Community with a specific mission of assisting Indians with legal problems. Kathy's support system has been personnel from a local Urban Indian Center. It appears her pursuit of a career created problems in her marriage. Her choice was to pursue her career even it if meant the dissolution of the marriage. Kathy experiences role strain as a single parent. She utilizes day care facilities and other support services for her children.

Summary

It can be seen from these vignettes that some Indian women are preparing for leadership roles while others are actively filling those roles. Culture is a significant factor in two areas. One, accepting the assignment of the female role of homemaker but also in providing the cause for a leadership role. Education is important to provide options for Indian women to the traditional homemaker role, or in conjunction with the homemaker role.

Indian women demonstrate a resilience and exceptional ability to adapt. They found support systems and maintained their cultural heritage while living in two worlds. They are making significant contributions to the Indian Nation through a combination of roles which are often in conflict. They are pursuing careers in social work, law, and local politics, yet they teach the cultural heritage to their children, and they provide role models for their children and other women.

To a great extent these women are experiencing similar role conflicts as women in the dominant society. They have, however, reduced feelings of guilt and shame in the deemphasis on homemaking by identifying the <u>need</u> for Indian leadership for both male and female in several areas. This is a response to oppressive external forces which threaten the survival of the American Indian Tribal System and the preservation of cultural traditions.

These case vignettes are evidence of a growing self-awareness and self-assessment current among Indian women today. It is part of the larger issue of individual autonomy in a multicultural society. For these women it means a different type of self actualization and expression of potential than the restricted avenues of the past. In some instances their activity could be compared to that of a religious or political leader who is willing to sacrifice everything for a cause.

Indian women are responding to external forces of oppression as well as internal forces crying for survival of a rich cultural tradition held holy and precious for thousands of years. Indian people are too small in number to restrict leadership to the male members. It is a time in history when Indian men and women must play many roles if they are to survive and keep intact their rich cultural heritage and their land base.

The Energy Crisis of the Twentieth Century has placed increased pressure on Indian Tribes holding valuable resources of oil, uranium and coal to give up their lands to the Federal Government or private interests.

The Longest Walk in 1978 from California to Washington, DC was a combined nation wide effort of tribes to gain support for the <u>Cause</u>. The participants in the Walk were men and women, young and old, who carried the pipe, Symbol of the Native American Spirit, across 3,000 miles of land which once sustained the buffalo herds, the soaring eagle and a people of habitual spiritual consciousness. The American Indian before contact with Europeans had attained perhaps the highest working concept of individualism ever practiced.

The changing roles of Indian women are in direct response to changes taking place within the local urban Indian community and on the national level. The decreasing number of eligible Indian men, increased educational opportunities, convenient day care facilities, concern for the health and welfare of Indian children, the elderly and national energy policies are all forces which shape the status and role of Indian women. The urban environment where other ethnic female role models live is also a force which inspires Indian women to be more active in community affairs in contrast to the former passive role of women on the reservation. Indian women are becoming more active but not to become liberated from Indian men. Their motivation is based once again upon survival of American Indians as a people. The goals of feminists is acknowledged to a lesser degree by urban Indian women.   They instead see their husbands as having fewer job opportunities than themselves in a white dominated society. Ethnic discrimination is a greater issue than sexual discrimination for Indian women. Indian women use their energy conservatively and thus far show little involvement in feminist movements.

Hopefully this article will be viewed as a bridge between two cultures. A means of broadening the comprehension of non-Indians of the tremendous price that American Indians have paid in the process of European colonization.

In addition it is hoped that the reader can catch a glimpse of where Indian women are today and where the new path leads.

"The truth comes into the world with two faces.
One is sad with suffering
and the other laughs.
It is the same face, laughing or weeping.
When people are already in despair,
maybe the laughing face is better for them."
(John G. Neihardt, Black Elk Speaks)

REFERENCES

Ablon, J. (1971). "Cultural Conflict in Urban Indians." MENTAL HYGIENE, 55(2), 199-205.

Coolidge, Dane (1977). "Kid Catching on the Navajo Reservation: 1930". THE DESTRUCTION OF AMERICAN INDIAN FAMILIES. New York: Association on American Indian Affairs.

Costo, Rupert and Henry, Jeannette (1977). INDIAN TREATIES: TWO CENTURIES OF DISHONOR. San Francisco: The Indian Historian Press.

Gridley, Marion (1974). NATIVE AMERICAN WOMEN. New York, New York: Hawthorne Books, Inc.

Hallowell, Irving (1925). "Ojibwa Personality and Acculturation." In ACCULTURATION IN THE AMERICAS. Vol. 2, 110.

La Pointe, James (1976). LEGENDS OF THE LAKOTA. San Francisco: The Indian Historian Press.

Mead, Margaret (1932). THE CHANGING CULTURE OF AN INDIAN TRIBE. New York, New York: Columbia University Press.

Medicine, Bea (1977). "Role and Function of Indian Women", INDIAN EDUCATION (National Indian Education Association), January.

Medicine, Bea (1978).   THE NATIVE AMERICAN WOMEN: A PERSPECTIVE. Austin, Texas: National Educational Laboratory Publishers, Inc.

Merian, Lewis (1977). "The Effects of Boarding Schools on Indian Family Life: 1928". THE DESTRUCTION OF AMERICAN INDIAN FAMILIES. New York: Association on American Indian Affairs.

Neihardt, John G. (1961). BLACK ELK SPEAKS. Lincoln, Nebraska: University of Nebraska Press.

Stuart, P. (1977). "United States Indian Policy" SOCIAL SERVICE REVIEW, September, 451-463.

United States Department of Commerce, Bureau of Census (1970). SUBJECT REPORT, AMERICAN INDIANS. Washington, DC: Government Printing Office.

7. AMERICAN INDIAN CHILD WELFARE

"Let us put our minds together and see what kind of
life we can make for our children"
Chief Sitting Bull

Introduction

Congressional investigations of child custody proceedings involving American Indian children culminated in the passage of the Indian Child Welfare Act. A two-fold national policy is outlined in the Act which protects the best interests of Indian children and promotes tribal entities. This Act attempts to prevent the separation of Indian children from their families and tribal heritage.

This section includes a copy of the Indian Child Welfare Act of 1978 and outlines the events leading up to the passage of the Act, discusses the role of the social worker in all aspects of Indian child welfare, and points out the role of social work education and training needs of social workers involved in services to American Indian populations.

Historical Review

The training and educational needs in the field of Indian Child Welfare can be traced to many years of federal policy intended toward the defeat of tribalism and the conquering and Christianizing of American Indians with the goal of assimilation into the dominant American society. In the process of colonization, American Indian families were chased westward and either captured or killed. In 1830 - 1870 the policy was extermination. The policy was later changed to segregate Indians by forcing them to live on desolate and barren parcels of land called reservations (Unger, 1977).

By 1875 a tremendous assault on Indians took place when Indian children in large numbers were placed in boarding schools long distances from their homes. The purpose was to deculturize, de-Indianize and separate Indian children from their parents and basically destroy tribal life. During these years of forced acculturation, traditional tribal parenting was disturbed and in some instances destroyed. The inter-generational effect of the boarding school era is still considered one of the major factors in the breakdown of Indian family traditions and has had a major impact on parenting practices for generations (Cross, 1986; Hull, 1982 Fischler, 1985).

With the passage of the Indian Re-Organization Act in the 1930's a radical move took place to protect and strengthen the tribal rights to exist. At this time Indian parents were writing letters to Congress and the President of the United States, complaining of the removal of children and their placement in military type boarding schools. Some children spent as many as fifteen years in these institutions if they were shipped long distances from home and had no immediate family.

By the 1950-1960's the Child Welfare League of America was contracting with the Bureau of Indian Affairs in carrying out the adoption of thousands of Indian children by non-Indian families. Racism was the dynamic for these widespread adoptions and foster placements of Indians in non-Indian homes. Indian children growing up in non-Indian homes became non-persons. They were raised in white homes but were never accepted by whites as socially appropriate candidates for dating or marriage to white partners. These children had no connection to their own culture and were rejected by the white culture. Later as adults, they developed mental health problems and substance abuse problems as they searched for an Indian identity and a positive self-image. In the 1950's the federal policies toward Indians emphasized termination of tribes, relocation to cities and assimilation of Indians into society as a means of destruction of the tribal cultures.

Transracial Adoptions

In reviewing the literature on American Indian transracial adoptions it was found to be detrimental to Indian children in the long run. Fanshel's study (1972) Far From the Reservation under the auspices of the Child Welfare League of America, (an agency which carried out widespread transracial adoptions of Indian children in the 50's through the 70's) states in his conclusion "It is my belief that ONLY the Indian people have the right to determine whether their children can be placed in white homes" (p. 218).

In 1981, Rita Simon and Howard Alstein conducted a five (5) year follow up study of 142 transracial adoptions of American Indian and African American children. They found 20-25% of these children had problems directly related to the transracial adoption. These children were stealing, running away and manifesting identity problems. Piliavin (1987) in a survey of homeless Indians in Minneapolis, Minnesota found early childhood non-Indian placement linked to homelessness, at twice the rate for the never homeless. In a recent survey of homeless American Indian males in Oakland and San Francisco, California, almost 99% of 40 subjects interviewed had experienced early childhood placements either in non-Indian foster homes, group homes or boarding schools (DuBray, 1992).

Simon and Alstein (1981) listed the responses to transracial adoption by neighbors, relatives, friends and grandparents which had a very negative impact on the American Indian or African American adopted child. Some 35% of adoptive parents reported that most of their close relatives assumed a negative and disapproving stance regarding the adoption. Another 31% of adoptive parents stated that their close relatives rejected the adopted children and were not reconciled with their parents. Grandparents were initially shocked, hostile and rejecting to the adopted child of color. Their general attitude, over time, did not change, as expressed in the language they used in reference to African Americans as "niggers" and to Asians as "gooks" or "chinks". They continued to make derogatory remarks about the laziness, dumbness, untrustworthiness, and so on, of such people. Approximately 12% of the adoptive parents reported that the rift over transracial adoption continued. Family ties had been broken and children of color felt responsible. Much tension over transracial adoption remained in these families (Simon and Alstein, 1981, p. 19).

Adoptive parents became more aware of how prejudiced they had been and, to some extent still were (p. 21). An adoptive father wrote about his 12 year old Indian son, "An ideal situation for him would include lots of space, trees and fields, animals and places to be active and/or quiet" (p. 21).

Some 20% of the adoptive parents were concerned that the adoption had caused marital strains. Marital problems were connected to acting out behavior of the adopted child such as the child lying, stealing, cheating, doing badly in school and being antagonistic and sullen at home.

The Child Welfare League in 1978, Standards for Adoption Service states (after the Indian Child Welfare Act was passed) "It is preferable to place a child in a family of his own racial background" (Simon & Alstein, 1981, p. 59).

American Indians must challenge the idea that there are insufficient Indian adoptive parents willing to adopt Indian children. Indians have historically adopted informally within extended family. There is no data available (longitudinal outcomes) to show that transracial adoption of Indian children outweighs the known disadvantages of an institution or foster care. Nor is there data to substantiate that transracial adoption of Indian children is in the best interest of the child.

The author has found (in 20 years of clinical experience working with American Indian populations) early childhood placement of American Indian children in non-Indian homes to have a devastating effect on the development of a healthy identity. These children suffer from a loss of self esteem and confused identity. They are ashamed of identifying as American Indian. They fail to achieve their academic potential, lack self-confidence, have high suicide rates of 70 per 100,000 (4 times the US rate for all races) and have a strong sense of alienation (Johnson, 1991). They also have high rates of substance abuse, depression, anxiety disorders and high rates of homelessness as adults (DuBray, 1992). Most of these children grow up with no connection to their Tribal culture, traditions, values and philosophy.

Non-Indians are not successful in transmitting Indian values, philosophy and culture to children because they have not experienced the culture. Much of what is taught in the culture is taught experientially, by participating in the family traditions, tribal ceremonies and teaching of the elders. Values are taught through the everyday behavior of the parent figures, aunts, uncles, grandparents and spiritual leaders. These things cannot be learned from reading a book. Social mannerisms are taught by modeling.

Non-Indians have taken adopted Indian children to Pow Wows where they observe the dancing and singing with no understanding of the meaning of each song, dance or the regalia worn by the dancers. Non-Indians are not sensitive to racial slurs that are offensive to Indians and thus never make the correction for the child. Most events in Indian cultures are symbolic and one must understand the symbolism in order to understand or teach the young. Most of this information is subtle and is never published in books. It is passed from one generation to the next through the oral tradition.

Anglo-American parents, no matter how liberal or well intended, cannot teach an Indian child how to survive in an essentially racist society. Anglo-Americans as adoptive parents cannot experience non-white status and are therefore not capable of understanding and coping with the racism that exists in American society. Since children tend to acquire most of the psychological and social characteristics of the families and communities in which they are reared, it is therefore possible that Indian children reared in white families and communities will develop anti-Indian psychological and social characteristics and thus develop serious identity problems in later life.

For too many years non-Indian child welfare workers have interpreted a lack of material wealth with a poverty of values or a poverty of affection when making decisions about American Indian families.

Indian Child Welfare Act

In 1967 the Association on American Indian Affairs in New York began investigations into the frequency of placement of Indians into non-Indian homes. The rates of non-Indian placement varied from 25% in some tribes to 100% in other tribes. The Indian Child Welfare Act commenced in 1967. After eleven years of investigations and congressional hearings the bill authored by James Abourezk, senator from South Dakota, was signed into law by President Carter in 1978. Every part of the Act addresses specific problems existing in Indian country. The heart of the law is the intention of keeping Indian children with their families and within the Indian community. There is no other law like it in the United States. The law regards tribal culture and customs as of paramount importance. The law is an attempt to tip the balance in court proceedings in favor of the tribes.

The law has been poorly implemented due to:

1. Insufficient funding levels for tribal programs.
2. The failure of federal and state agencies to implement adequate rehabilitative programs for Indian parents and families.
3. Continued unlawful practices by state child protection services toward Indians.
4. A lack of emphasis on the Indian Child Welfare Act in the education of social workers throughout the country.

The 1990's

Today, hundreds of years after the trauma of wars of resistance, relocation and forced acculturation in boarding schools, the inter-generational scars can be clearly observed as a major factor in the social, spiritual and emotional problems present in Indian country. Many Indian people are searching for their cultural identity as they come in conflict with the values of a dominant society which places materialism, competition and greed for power as the top priorities of the day. Racism remains the underlying dynamic in many practices toward American Indians as Indians stand between the land and those who want more land (DuBray, 1985).

There are many unmet needs within the Indian communities for relevant mental health services for youth and families. There is a need for treatment and healing of adults and children who have been physically and sexually abused in federally funded boarding schools. There are unmet needs for effective treatment for substance abusers who experienced early childhood placement and abandonment. There is a need for parenting skills for those descendants of the boarding school era. There is a great need for culturally sensitive child welfare services. There is a need for assistance in community development as tribes move toward addressing problems of substance abuse and domestic violence from a community approach incorporating spirituality. The schools of social work education can assist American Indians in many areas by linking with tribal programs and recruitment of Indian students interested in a social work career.

The Role of the Child Welfare Social Worker

Social workers are involved in all aspects of Indian child welfare including protective services, removal, placement and adoptions. With the growth of social service protective services and the development of advocacy roles, many social workers are spending more of their time preparing court documents. Family evaluations are increasing because court cases on children and parents are increasing. It is no longer sufficient to just establish neglect or abuse; the "right" to treatment and rehabilitation requires social workers to be actively involved.

Following are five major roles of social workers in the courts. The needs of the court dictate the extent to which any one social worker plays the role alone or jointly with others.

1.   Petitioner

A petition to remove the child from his parents under mandate of the "society's interest" to protect children through court action is customarily filed by the social worker.

2.   Defendant

The social worker may have to answer charges for an agency that is being sued and also occasionally may be named personally as a co-defendant. An example would be a suit by a foster parent requesting the court to restrain the agency and the social worker from removing the child.

3.   Expert Witness

Because of his/her knowledge and experience in child welfare, a social worker may appear on behalf of a child or parent for very specific issues.

4.   Client Advocate

A social worker may explain the problems of the child or parent to justify behavior(s) or to place in needed services.

5.   Resource

The social worker functions as a resource of the court staff to aid in fact-finding and treatment and is then responsible for court report(s) upon which a disposition is based.

Role Conflicts of Social Workers

According to the National Indian Justice Center in Petaluma, California (1978), the following problem areas concern social workers:

Social workers do not know the rules on due process and the difference between facts and hearsay.

Social workers dislike resolving problems by adversary techniques. They would prefer case conferences and consensus.

Social workers feel lawyers avoid reconciliation.

Social workers see judges as advocates for the parent, causing the social worker to defend the child and appear against the parents.

Social workers may have difficulty establishing sound legal basis for their recommendations.

Social workers play a central role in child abuse and neglect cases and they must interact with all of the others involved in the case. They have the greatest potential for role problems.

These issues need to be addressed in social work education to prepare future child welfare workers.

Implementation of the Indian Child Welfare Act

Schools of social work can play an important role in assisting in the implementation of the law by providing comprehensive education about the Act and raising the issues about implementation in the college classroom. In addition schools of social work can provide planned part-time MSW programs for staff employed in Indian Child Welfare Agencies who are in need of graduate education. Classes and weekend seminars can be brought to remote areas by closed circuit television and traveling faculty when there is a strong commitment to social work education. California State University, Sacramento has provided a Child and Family program of this nature in Northern California with great success.

Schools of social work can also provide seminars for Children's Protective Service Departments in county programs where the law is poorly implemented. There are no limits to the assistance schools of social work can provide when faculty are concerned about implementation of the law. The challenge then is to educate faculty of schools of social work on the importance of emphasizing the Indian Child Welfare Act in all concentrations within the social work major and provide curriculum to complete the task.

Faculty of schools of social work need to conduct research on effective interventions with abusive families. There is also a need for curriculum which better prepares social workers to function in the many roles required in managing child abuse cases involving the courts.

It is hoped that by improving the education of a new generation of social workers, the Indian Child welfare Act of 1978 will move toward implementation and American Indian tribes will again have jurisdiction over Indian child welfare matters.

The Indian Child Welfare Act of 1978

United States Code
Title 25, § 1901-1963

§ 1901. Congressional findings

Recognizing the special relationship between the United States and the Indian tribes and their members and the Federal responsibility to Indian people, the Congress finds--

(1) that clause 3, section 8, article I of the United States Constitution provides that "The Congress shall have Power...To regulate Commerce...with Indian tribes" and, through this and other constitutional authority, Congress has plenary power over Indian affairs;

(2) that Congress, through statutes, treaties, and the general course of dealing with Indian tribes, has assumed the responsibility for the protection and preservation of Indian tribes and their resources;

(3) that there is no resource that is more vital to the continued existence and integrity of Indian tribes than their children and that the United States has a direct interest, as trustee, in protecting Indian children who are members of or are eligible for membership in an Indian tribe;

(4) that an alarmingly high percentage of Indian families are broken up by the removal, often unwarranted, of their children from them by nontribal public and private agencies and that an alarmingly high percentage of such children are placed in non-Indian foster and adoptive homes and institutions; and

(5) that the States, exercising their recognized jurisdiction over Indian child custody proceedings through administrative and judicial bodies, have often failed to recognize the essential tribal relations of Indian people and the cultural and social standards prevailing in Indian communities and families.

Publ. L. 95-608, § 2, Nov. 8, 1978, 92 Stat. 3069.

§ 1902. Congressional declaration of policy

The Congress hereby declares that it is the policy of this Nation to protect the best interests of Indian children and to promote the stability and security of Indian tribes and families by the establishment of minimum Federal standards for the removal of Indian children from their families and the placement of such children in foster or adoptive homes which will reflect the unique values of Indian culture, and by providing for assistance to

Indian tribes in the operation of child and family service programs.
Pub. L. 95-608, § 3, Nov, 1978, 92 Stat. 3069.

§ 1903. Definitions

For the purposes of this chapter, except as may be specifically provided otherwise, the term--

(1) "child custody proceeding" shall mean and include--

(i) "foster care placement" which shall mean any action removing an Indian child from its parent or Indian custodian for temporary placement in a foster home or institution or the home of a guardian or conservator where the parent or Indian custodian cannot have the child returned upon demand, but where parental rights have not been terminated;

(ii) "termination of parental rights" which shall mean any action resulting in the termination of the parent-child relationship;

(iii) "preadoptive placement" which shall mean the temporary placement of an Indian child in a foster home or institution after the termination of parental rights, but prior to or in lieu of adoptive placement; and

(iv) "adoptive placement" which shall mean the permanent placement of an Indian child for adoption, including any action resulting in a final decree of adoption.

Such term or terms shall not include a placement based upon an act which, if committed by an adult, would be deemed a crime or upon an award, in a divorce proceeding, of custody to one of the parents.

(2) "extended family member" shall be defined by the law or custom of the Indian child's tribe or, in the absence of such law or custom, shall be a person who has reached the age of eighteen and who is the Indian child's grandparent, aunt or uncle, brother or sister, brother-in-law or sister-in-law, niece or nephew, first or second cousin, or stepparent;

(3) "Indian" means any person who is a member of an Indian tribe, or who is an Alaska Native and a member of a Regional Corporation as defined in section 1606 of Title 43;

(4) "Indian child" means any unmarried person who is under age eighteen and is either (a) a member of an Indian tribe or (b) is eligible for membership in an Indian tribe and is the biological child of a member of an Indian tribe;

(5) "Indian child's tribe" means (a) the Indian tribe in which an Indian child is a member or eligible for membership or (b), in the case of an Indian child who is a member of or eligible for membership in more than one tribe, the Indian tribe

with which the Indian child has the more significant contacts;

(6) "Indian custodian" means any Indian person who has legal custody of an Indian child under tribal law or custom or under State law or to whom temporary physical care, custody, and control has been transferred by the parent of such child;

(7) "Indian organization" means any group, association, partnership, corporation, or other legal majority of whose members are Indians;

(8) "Indian tribe" means any Indian tribe, band, nation, or other organized group or community of Indians recognized as eligible for the services provided to Indians by the Secretary because of their status as Indians, including any Alaska Native village as defined in section 1602(c) of Title 43;

(9) "parent" means any biological parent or parents of an Indian child or any Indian person who has lawfully adopted an Indian child, including adoptions under tribal law or custom. It does not include the unwed father where paternity has not been acknowledged or established;

(10) "reservation" means Indian country as defined in section 1151 of Title 18 and any lands, not covered under such section, title to which is either held by the United States in trust for the benefit of any Indian tribe or individual or held by any Indian tribe or individual subject to a restriction by the United States against alienation;

(11) "Secretary" means the Secretary of the Interior; and

(12) "tribal court" means a court with jurisdiction over child custody proceedings and which is either a Court of Indian Offenses, a court established and operated under the code or custom of an Indian tribe, or any other administrative body of a tribe which is vested with authority over child custody proceedings.
Publ. L. 95-608, § 4, Nov. 8, 1978, 92 Stat. 3069.

SUBCHAPTER 1 - Child Custody Proceedings

§ 1911. Indian tribe jurisdiction over Indian child custody proceedings--Exclusive jurisdiction.

(a) An Indian tribe shall have jurisdiction exclusive as to any State over any child custody proceeding involving and Indian child who resides or is domiciled within the reservation of such tribe, except where jurisdiction is otherwise vested in the State by existing Federal law. Where an Indian child is a ward of a tribal court, the Indian tribe shall retain exclusive jurisdiction, notwithstanding the residence or domicile of the child.

Transfer of proceedings: declination by tribal court.

(b) In any State court proceedings for the foster care placement of, or termination of parental rights to, an Indian child not domiciled or residing within the reservation of the Indian child's tribe, the court, in the absence of good cause to the contrary, shall transfer such proceeding to the jurisdiction of the tribe, absent objection by either parent, upon the petition of either parent or the Indian custodian or the Indian child's tribe: Provided, That such transfer shall be subject to declination by the tribal court of such tribe.

State court proceedings; intervention

(c) In any State court proceeding for the foster placement of, or termination of parental rights to, an Indian child, the Indian custodian of the child and the Indian child's tribe shall have a right to intervene at any point in the proceeding.

Full faith and credit to public acts, records and judicial proceedings of Indian tribes.

(d) The United States, every State, every territory or possession of the United States, and every Indian tribe shall give full faith and credit to the public acts, records, and judicial proceedings of any Indian tribe applicable to Indian child custody proceedings to the same extent that such entities give full faith and credit to the public acts, records, and judicial proceedings of any other entity.
Pub. L. 95-608, Title I, § see 7530. Title I, § 101, Nov. 8, 1978, 92 Stat. 3071.

§ 1912. Pending court proceedings--Notice; time for commencement of proceedings; additional time for preparation

(a) In any involuntary proceeding in a State court, where the court knows or has reason to know that an Indian child is involved, the party seeking the foster care placement of, or termination of parental rights to, an Indian child shall notify the parent or Indian custodian and the Indian child's tribe, by registered mail with return receipt request, of the pending proceedings and their right of intervention. If the identity or location of the parent or Indian custodian and the Indian child's tribe, by registered mail with return receipt requested, of the pending proceedings and of their right of intervention. If the identity or location of the parent or Indian custodian and the tribe cannot be determined, such notice shall be given to the Secretary in like manner, who shall have fifteen days after receipt to provide the requisite notice to the parent or Indian custodian and the tribe. No foster care placement or termination of parental rights proceeding shall be held until at least ten days after receipt of notice by the parent or Indian custodian and the tribe or the Secretary: Provided, That the parent or Indian custodian or the tribe shall, upon request, be granted up to twenty additional days to prepare for such proceeding.

Appointment of counsel

(b) In any case in which the court determines indigency, the parent or Indian custodian shall have the right to court-appointed counsel in any removal, placement, or termination proceeding. The court may, in its discretion, appoint counsel for the child upon a finding that such appointment is in the best interest of the child. Where State law makes no provision for appointment of counsel in such proceedings, the court shall promptly notify the Secretary upon appointment of counsel, and the Secretary, upon certification of the presiding judge, shall pay reasonable fees and expenses out of funds which may be appropriated pursuant to section 13 of this title.

Examination of reports or other documents

(c) Each party to a foster care placement or termination of parental rights proceeding under State law involving an Indian child shall have the right to examine all reports or other documents filed with the court upon which any decision with respect to such action may be based.

Remedial services and rehabilitative programs; preventive measures

(d) Any party seeking to effect a foster care placement of, or termination of parental rights to, an Indian child under State law shall satisfy the court that active efforts have been made to provide remedial services and rehabilitative programs designed to prevent the breakup of the Indian family and that these efforts have proved unsuccessful.

Foster care placement orders; evidence; determination of damage to child

(d) No foster care placement may be ordered in such proceeding in the absence of a determination, supported by clear and convincing evidence, including testimony of qualified expert witnesses, that the continued custody of the child by the parent or Indian custodian is likely to result in serious emotional or physical damage to the child.

Parental rights termination orders; evidence; determination of damage to child.

(f) No termination of parental rights may be ordered in such proceeding in the absence of a determination, supported by evidence beyond a reasonable doubt, including testimony of qualified expert witnesses, that the continued custody of the child by the parent or Indian custodian is likely to result in serious emotional or physical damage to the child.
Pub. L. 95-608, Title I, § 102, Nov, 1978, 92 Stat. 3071.

§ 1913. Parental rights, voluntary termination--Consent; record; certification matters; invalid consents

(a) Where any parent or Indian custodian voluntarily consents to a foster care placement or to termination of parental right, such consent shall not be valid unless executed in writing and recorded before a judge of a court of competent jurisdiction and accompanied by the presiding judge's certificate that the terms and consequences of the consent were fully explained in detail and were fully understood by the parent or Indian custodian. The court shall also certify that either the parent or Indian custodian fully understood the explanation in English or that it was interpreted into a language that the parent or Indian custodian understood. Any consent given prior to, or within ten days after, birth of the Indian child shall not be valid.

Foster care placement; withdrawal of consent

(b) Any parent or Indian custodian may withdraw consent to a foster care placement under State law at any time and, upon such withdrawal, the child shall be returned to the parent or Indian custodian.

Voluntary termination of parental rights or adoptive placement,: withdrawal of consent; return of custody

(c) In any voluntary proceeding for termination of parental rights, to or adoptive placement of, an Indian child, the consent of the parent may be withdrawn for any reason at any time prior to the entry of a final decree of termination or adoption, as the case may be, and the child shall be returned to the parent.

Collateral attack; vacation of decree and return of custody; limitations

(d) After the entry of a final decree of adoption of an Indian child in any State court, the parent may withdraw consent thereto upon the grounds that consent was obtained through fraud or duress and may petition the court to vacate such decree. Upon a finding that such consent was obtained through fraud or duress, the court shall vacate such decree and return the child to the parent. No adoption which has been effective for at least two years may be invalidated under the provisions of this subsection unless otherwise permitted under State law.
Pub. L. 95-608, Title I, § 103, Nov, 1978, 92 Stat. 3072.

§ 1914. Petition to court of competent jurisdiction to invalidate action upon showing of certain violations.

Any Indian child who is the subject of any action for foster care placement or termination of parental rights under State law, any parent or Indian custodian from whose custody such child was removed, and the Indian child's tribe may petition any court of competent jurisdiction to invalidate such action upon a showing that such action violated any provision of 1911, 1912, and 1913 of this title.
Pub. L. 95-608, Title I, § 104, Nov. 8, 1978, 92 Stat. 3072.

§ 1915. Placement of Indian children--Adoptive placements; preferences

(a) In any adoptive placement of an Indian child under State law, a preference shall be given, in the absence of good cause to the contrary, to a placement with (1) a member of the child's extended family; (2) other members of the Indian child's tribe; or (3) other Indian families.

Foster care or preadoptive placements; criteria; preferences

(b) Any child accepted for foster care or preadoptive placement shall be placed in the least restrictive setting which most approximates a family in which his special needs, if any, may be met. The child shall also be placed within reasonable proximity to his or her home, taking into account any special needs of the child. In any foster care or preadoptive placement, a preference shall be given, in the absence of good cause to the contrary, to a placement with--

(i) a member of the Indian child's extended family;

(ii) a foster home licensed, approved, or specified by the Indian child's tribe;

(iii) an Indian foster home licensed by an authorized non-Indian licensing authority; or

(iv) an institution for children approved by an Indian tribe or operated by an Indian organization which has a program suitable to meet the Indian child's needs.

Tribal resolution for different order of preference; personal preference considered; anonymity in application of preferences

(c) In the case of placement under subsection (1) or (b) of this section, if the Indian child's tribe shall establish a different order of preference by resolution, the agency or court effecting the placement shall follow such order so long as the placement is the least restrictive setting appropriate to the particular needs of the child, as provided in subsection (b) of this section. Where appropriate, the preference of the Indian child or parent shall be considered: Provided, That where a consenting parent evidences a desire for anonymity, the court or agency shall give weight to such desire in applying the preferences.

Social and cultural standards applicable

(d) The standards to be applied in meeting the preference requirements of this section shall be the prevailing social and cultural standards of the Indian community in which the parent or extended family resides or with which the parent or extended family members maintain social and cultural ties.

Record of placement; availability

(e) A record of each such placement, under State law, of an Indian child shall be maintained by the State in which the placement was made, evidencing the efforts to comply with the order of preferences specified in this section. Such record shall be made available at any time upon the request of the Secretary or the Indian child's tribe.
Pub. L. 95-608, Title I, § 105, Nov. 8, 1978, 92 Stat. 3073.

§ 1916. Return of custody--Petition; best interests of child

(a) Notwithstanding State law to the contrary, whenever a final decree of adoption of an Indian child has been vacated or set aside or the adoptive parents voluntarily consent to the termination of their parental rights to the child, a biological parent or prior Indian custodian may petition for return of custody and the court shall grant such petition unless there is a showing, in the proceeding subject to the provisions of section 1912 of this title, that such return or custody is not in the best interests of the child.

Removal from foster care home; placement procedure

(b) Whenever an Indian child is removed from a foster care home or institution for the purpose of further foster care, preadoptive, or adoptive placement, such placement shall be in accordance with the provisions of this chapter, except in the case where an Indian child is being returned to the parent or Indian custodian from whose custody the child was originally removed.
Pub. L. 95-608, Title I, § 106, Nov. 8, 1978, 72 Stat. 3703.

§ 1917. Tribal affiliation information and other information for protection of rights from tribal relationship; application of subject of adoptive placement; disclosure by court

Upon application by an Indian individual who has reached the age of eighteen and who was the subject of an adoptive placement, the court which entered the final decree shall inform such individual of the tribal affiliation, if any, of the individual's biological parents and provide such other information as may be necessary to protect any rights flowing from the individual's tribal relationship.
Pub. L. 95-608, Title I, § 107, Nov. 8, 1978, 92 Stat. 3703.

§ 1918. Reassumption jurisdiction over child custody proceedings--Petition; suitable plan; approval by Secretary

(a) Any Indian tribe which became subject to State jurisdiction pursuant to the provisions of the Act of August 15, 1953 (67 Stat. 588), as amended by subchapter III of chapter 15 of this title, or pursuant to any other Federal law, may reassume jurisdiction over child custody proceedings. Before any Indian tribe may reassume jurisdiction over Indian child custody proceedings, such tribe shall present to the Secretary for approval a petition to reassume such jurisdiction which includes a suitable plan to exercise such jurisdiction.

Criteria applicable to consideration by Secretary; partial retrocession

(b)(1) In considering the petition and feasibility of the plan of a tribe under subsection (a) of this section, the Secretary may consider, among other things:

(i)   whether or not the tribe maintains a membership roll or alternative provision for clearly identifying the persons who will be affected by the reassumption of jurisdiction by the tribe;

(ii) the size of the reservation or former reservation area which will be affected by retrocession and reassumption of jurisdiction by the tribe;

(iii) the population base of the tribe, or distribution of the population in homogeneous communities or geographic areas; and

(iv) the feasibility of the plan in cases of multitribal occupation of a single reservation or geographic area.

(2) In those cases where the Secretary determines that the jurisdictional provisions of section 1911(a) of this title are not feasible, he is authorized to accept partial retrocession which will enable tribes to exercise referral jurisdiction as provided in section 1911(b) of this title, or, where appropriate, will allow them to exercise exclusive jurisdiction as provided in section 1911(a) of this title over limited community or geographic areas without regard for the reservation status of the area affected.

Approval of petition; publication in Federal Register; notice; reassumption period; correction of causes for disapproval

(c) If the Secretary approves any petition under subsection (a) of this section, the Secretary shall publish notice of such approval in the Federal Register and shall notify the affected State or States of such approval. The Indian tribe concerned shall reassume jurisdiction sixty days after publication in the Federal Register of notice of approval. If the Secretary disapproves any petition under subsection (a) of this section, the Secretary shall provide such technical assistance as may be necessary to enable the tribe to correct any deficiency which the Secretary identified as a cause for disapproval.

Pending actions or proceedings unaffected

(d) Assumption of jurisdiction under this section shall not affect any action or proceeding over which a court has already assumed jurisdiction, except as may be provided pursuant to any agreement under section 1919 of this title.
Pub. L. 95-608, Title I, § 108, Nov. 8, 1978, 92 Stat. 3704.

§ 1919. Agreements between States and Indian tribes--Subject coverage

(a) States and Indian tribes are authorized to enter into agreements with each other respecting care and custody of Indian children and jurisdiction over child custody proceedings, including agreements which may provide for orderly transfer of jurisdiction on a case-by-case basis and agreements which provide for concurrent jurisdiction between States and Indian tribes.

Revocation; notice; actions or proceedings unaffected

(b) Such agreements may be revoked by either party upon one hundred and eighty days' written notice to the other party. Such revocation shall not affect any action or proceeding over which a court has already assumed jurisdiction, unless the agreement

provides otherwise.
Pub. L. 95-608, Title I, § 109, Nov. 8, 1978, 92 Stat. 3074.

§ 1920.   Improper removal of child from custody; declination of jurisdiction; forthwith
return of child: danger exception
     Where any petitioner in an Indian child custody proceeding before a State court has improperly removed the child from custody of the parent or Indian custodian or has improperly retained custody after a visit or other temporary relinquishment of custody, the court shall decline jurisdiction over such petition and shall forthwith return the child to his parent or Indian custodian unless returning the child to his parent or custodian would subject the child to a substantial and immediate danger or threat of such danger.
Pub. L. 95-608, Title I, § 110, Nov. 8, 1978, 92 Stat. 3075.

§ 1921.   Higher State or Federal standard applicable to protect rights of parent or Indian
custodian of Indian child
     In any case where State or Federal law applicable to a child custody proceeding under State or Federal law provides a higher standard of protection to the rights of the parent or Indian custodian of an Indian child than the rights provided under this subchapter, the State or Federal court shall apply the State or Federal standard.
Pub. L. 95-608, Title I, § 111, Nov. 8, 1978, 92 Stat. 3075.

§ 1922.   Emergency removal or placement of child; termination; appropriate action
     Nothing in this subchapter shall be construed to prevent the emergency removal of an Indian child who is a resident of or is domiciled on a reservation, but temporarily located off the reservation, from his parent or Indian custodian or the emergency placement of such child in a foster home or institution, under applicable State law, in order to prevent imminent physical damage or harm to the child. The State authority, official, or agency involved shall insure that the emergency removal or placement terminates immediately when such removal or placement is no longer necessary to prevent imminent physical damage or harm to the child and shall expeditiously initiate a child custody proceeding subject to the provisions of this subchapter, transfer the child to the jurisdiction of the appropriate Indian tribe, or restore the child to the parent or Indian custodian, as may be appropriate.
Pub. L. 95-608, Title I, § 112, Nov. 8, 1978, 92 Stat. 3075.

§ 1923.   Effective date
     None of the provisions of this subchapter, except sections 1911(a), 1918, and 1919 of this title, shall affect a proceeding under State law for foster care placement, termination of parental rights, preadoptive placement, or adoptive placement which was initiated or completed prior to one hundred and eighty days after November 8, 1978, but shall apply

to any subsequent proceeding in the same manner or subsequent proceedings affecting the custody or placement of the same child.
Pub. L. 95-608, Title I, § 113, Nov. 8, 1978, 92 Stat. 3075.

SUBCHAPTER II - Indian Child and Family Programs

§ 1931. Grants for on or near reservation programs and child welfare codes--Statement of purpose; scope of programs

(a) The Secretary is authorized to make grants to Indian tribes and organizations in the establishment and operation of Indian child and family service programs on or near reservations and in the preparation and implementation of child welfare codes. The objective of every Indian child and family service program shall be to prevent the breakup of Indian families and, in particular, to insure that the permanent removal of an Indian child from the custody of his parent or Indian custodian shall be a last resort. Such child and family service programs may include, but are not limited to--

(1) a system for licensing or otherwise regulating Indian foster and adoptive homes;

(2) the operation and maintenance of facilities for the counseling and treatment of Indian families and for the temporary custody of Indian children;

(3) family assistance, including homemaker and home counselors, day care, afterschool care, and employment, recreational activities, and respite care;

(4) home improvement programs;

(5) the employment of professional and other trained personnel to assist the tribal court in the disposition of domestic relations and child welfare matters;

(6) education and training of Indians, including tribal court judges and staff, in skills relating to child and family assistance and service programs;

(7) a subsidy program under which Indian adoptive children may be provided support comparable to that for which they would be eligible as foster children, taking into account the appropriate State standards of support for maintenance and medical needs; and

(8) guidance, legal representation, and advice to Indian families involved in tribal, State, or Federal child custody proceedings.

Non-Federal matching funds for related Social Security or other Federal financial assistance programs; assistance for such programs unaffected; State licensing or approval for qualification for assistance under federally assisted program

(b) Funds appropriated for use by the Secretary in accordance with this section may be utilized as non-Federal matching share in connection with funds provided under titles IV-B and XX of the Social Security Act or under any other Federal financial assistance

programs which contribute to the purpose for which such funds are authorized to be appropriated for use under this chapter. The provision or possibility of assistance under this chapter shall not be a basis for the denial or reduction of any assistance otherwise authorized under titles IV-B and XX of the Social Security Act or any other federally assisted program. For purposes of qualifying for assistance under a federally assisted program, licensing or approval of foster or adoptive homes or institutions by an Indian tribe shall be deemed equivalent to licensing or approval by a State.
Pub. L. 95-608, Title II, § 201, Nov. 8, 1978, 92 Stat. 3075.

§ 1932. Grants for off-reservation programs for additional services
    The Secretary is also authorized to make grants to Indian organizations to establish and operate off-reservation Indian child and family service programs which may include, but are not limited to--
        (1) a system for regulating, maintaining, and supporting Indian foster and adoptive homes, including a subsidy program under which Indian adoptive children may be provided support comparable to that for which they would be eligible as Indian foster children, taking into account the appropriate State standards of support for maintenance and medical needs;
        (2) the operation and maintenance of facilities and services for counseling and treatment of Indian families and Indian foster and adoptive children;
        (3) family assistance, including homemaker and home counselors, day care, afterschool care, and employment, recreational activities, and respite care; and
        (4) guidance, legal representation, and advice to Indian families involved in chid custody proceedings.
Pub. L. 96-608, Title II, § 202, Nov. 8, 1978, 92 Stat. 3076.

§ 1933. Funds for on and off reservation programs--Appropriated funds for similar programs of Department of Health, Education, and Welfare; appropriation in advance for payments
    (a) In the establishment, operation, and funding of Indian child and family service programs, both on and off reservation, the Secretary may enter into agreements with the Secretary of Health, Education, and Welfare, and the latter Secretary is hereby authorized for such purposes to use funds appropriated for similar programs of the Department of Health, Education and Welfare: Provided, That authority to make payments pursuant to such agreements shall be effective only to the extent and such amount as may be provided in advance by appropriation Acts.

Appropriation authorization under section 13 of this title
    (b) Funds for the purposes of this chapter may be appropriated pursuant to the provisions of section 13 of this title.
Pub. L. 95-608, Title II, § 203, Nov. 8, 1978, 92 Stat. 3076.

§ 1034. "Indian" defined for certain purposes

For the purposes of sections 1932 and 1933 of this title, the term "Indian" shall includes persons defined in section 1603(c) of this title.
Pub. L. 95-608, Title II, § 204, Nov. 8, 1978, 92 Stat. 3077.

SUBCHAPTER III -- Recordkeeping, Information Availability and Timetables

§ 1951. Information availability to and disclosure by Secretary--Copy of final decree or order; other information; anonymity affidavit; exemption from Freedom of Information Act

(a) Any State court entering a final decree in ordering any Indian child adoptive placement after November 8, 1978, shall provide the Secretary with a copy of such decree or order together with such other information as may be necessary to show--

(1) the names and tribal affiliation of the child;

(2) the names and addresses of the biological parents;

(3) the names and addresses of the adoptive parents; and

(4) the identity of any agency having files or information relating to such adoptive placement.

Where the court records contain an affidavit of the biological parent or parents that their identity remain confidential, the court shall include such affidavit with the other information. The Secretary shall insure that the confidentiality of such information is maintained and such information shall not be subject to the Freedom of Information Act, as amended

Disclosure of Information for enrollment of Indian child in tribe or for determination of member rights or benefits; certification of entitlement to enrollment

(b) Upon the request of the adopted Indian child over the age of eighteen, the adoptive or foster parents of an Indian child, or an Indian tribe, the Secretary shall disclose such information as may be necessary for the enrollment of an Indian child in the tribe in which the child may be eligible for enrollment or for determining any rights or benefits associated with that membership. Where the documents relating to such child contain an affidavit from the biological parent or parents requesting anonymity, the Secretary shall certify to the Indian child's tribe, where the information warrants, that the child's parentage and other circumstances of birth entitle the child to enrollment under the criteria established by such tribe.
Pub. L. 95-608, Title III, § 301, Nov. 8, 1978, 92 Stat. 3077.

§ 1952. Rules and Regulations

Within one hundred and eighty days after November 8, 1978, the Secretary shall promulgate such rules and regulations as may be necessary to carry out the provisions of

this chapter.
Pub. L. 95-608, Title III, § 302, Nov. 8, 1978, 92 Stat. 3077.

SUBCHAPTER IV -- Miscellaneous Provisions

§ 1961.   Education; day schools, report to congressional committees; particular consideration of elementary grade facilities
(a)   It is the sense of Congress that the absence of locally convenient day schools may contribute to the breakup of Indian families.
(b)   The Secretary is authorized and directed to prepare, in consultation with appropriate agencies in the Department of Health, Education and Welfare, a report on the feasibility of providing Indian children with schools located near their homes, and to submit such report to the Select Committee on Indian Affairs of the United States Senate and the Committee on Interior and Insular Affairs of the United States House of Representatives within two years from November 8, 1978. In developing this report the Secretary shall give particular consideration to the provision of educational facilities for children in the elementary grades.
Pub. L. 95-608, Title IV, § 401, Nov. 8, 1978, 92 Stat. 3078.

§ 1962. Copies to the States
Within sixty days after November 8, 1978, the Secretary shall send to the Governor, chief justice of the highest court of appeal, and the attorney general of each State a copy of this chapter, together with committee reports and an explanation of the provisions of this chapter.
Pub. L. 95-608, Title IV, § 402, Nov. 8, 1978, 92 Stat. 3078.

§ 1963. Severability of provisions
If any provision of this chapter or the applicability thereof is held invalid, the remaining provisions of this chapter shall not be affected thereby.
Pub. L. 95-608, Title IV, § 403, Nov. 8, 1978, 92 Stat. 3078.

REFERENCES

CHILD ABUSE AND NEGLECT (1987), Legal Education Series, National Indian   Justice Center, Petaluma, CA.

Cross, T.L. (1986). Drawing on Cultural Tradition in Indian Child Welfare   Practice. SOCIAL CASEWORK, 67, 283-289.

DuBray, Wynne Hanson (1985). American Indian Values: Critical Factor in   Casework SOCIAL CASEWORK, 66, 30-37.

DuBray, Wynne Hanson (1992). HOMELESS AMERICAN INDIAN MALES, In   Press.

Fischler, R.S. (1985). Child Abuse and Neglect in American Indian   Communities. CHILD ABUSE AND NEGLECT, 9 (1), 95-106.

Hull, G.H. (1982). Child Welfare Services to Native Americans, SOCIAL CASEWORK, 340-347.

Johnson, Troy E., (1991). CONFERENCE PROCEEDINGS OF INDIAN CHILD   WELFARE CONFERENCE, American Indian Studies Center, UCLA.

Piliavin, Irivng, Sosin, Michael, Westerfelt, Herb (1990). Conditions Contribution to Long-term Homelessness: An Exploratory Study. IRP Discussion Paper No. 853-87. Madison: University of Wisconsin Institute of Research on Poverty.

Simon, Rita J. and Alstein, Howard, (1981). TRANSRACIAL ADOPTION: A FOLLOW UP, Lexington Books, Lexington, MA.

Unger, Steven (1977).   THE DESTRUCTION OF AMERICAN INDIAN FAMILIES. Association on American Indian Affairs, Inc., New York, New York.

BIBLIOGRAPHY

Human Behavior and American Indians

HUMAN BEHAVIOR BIBLIOGRAPHY

Abel, Annie Heloise (1972), THE HISTORY OF EVENTS RESULTING IN INDIAN CONSOLIDATION WEST OF THE MISSISSIPPI, AMS Press, New York.

Aberle, David (1957). NAVAJO & UTE PEYOTISM: A CHRONOLOGICAL & DISTRIBUTIONAL STUDY, University of Colorado Press, Boulder, Colorado.

Adams, Evelyn C. (1971), AMERICAN INDIAN EDUCATION, Arno Press and the N.Y. Times, NY.

Adams, John (1973), THE GITKSAN POTLATCH, Holt, Rinehart & Winston of Canada, Limited, Toronto, Montreal.

Adams, Richard C. (1904), THE ANCIENT RELIGION OF THE DELAWARE INDIANS & OBSERVATIONS AND REFLECTIONS, The Law Reporter Printing Co., Washington, DC.

Adams, William Y. & Ruffing, Lorraine T. (Univ. of Kentucky, Lexington) (March 1977), "Shonto Revisited: Measures of Social and Economic Change in a Navajo Community," 1955-1971, AMERICAN ANTHROPOLOGIST, 79, 1, p. 58-83.

ADVISORY COUNCIL ON THE ELDERLY AMERICAN INDIAN (1971), "A Statement by the Council," Washington, DC, U.S. Government Printing Press, November.

Aginsky, Burt & Ethel (1976), DEEP VALLEY, (Pomo Way of Life), Stein & Day Publishers, N.Y.

Aikens, C. Melvin (1971), GREAT BASIN ANTHROPOLOGICAL CONFERENCE 1970, University of Oregon Press.

Akwesasne Notes, (1974), VOICES FROM WOUNDED KNEE 1973, Rooseveltown, N.Y.

Alexander, Hartley (1953), THE WORLD'S RIM, GREAT MYSTERIES OF THE NORTH AMERICAN INDIANS, University of Nebraska Press, Lincoln, Nebraska.

Allen, Michael A. (1974), "A Profile of Needs and Recommendations for Implementing Aging Programs on Ten Arizona Reservations," Bureau on Aging, Arizona Department of Economic Security.

American Anthropologist (1960), SELECTED PAPERS FROM THE AMERICAN ANTHROPOLOGIST, 1888-1920, Row, Peterson & Co., Evanston, Illinois.

American Ethnological Society, AMS Press, New York, Volumes on different tribes and culture. (N.A.S. Library, U.C.B.).

American Indian Reader (1972), Rupert Costo, HISTORY, The Indian Historian Press, Inc., San Francisco.

Jeanette Henry (1972), ANTHROPOLOGY, The Indian Historian Press, Inc., San Francisco.

American Indian Reader, Jeannette Henry (1974), EDUCATION, The Indian Historian Press, Inc., San Francisco.

American Indian Health Series (1974). Melvin Lee, DIAGNOSIS & TREATMENT OF PREVALENT DISEASES OF NORTH AMERICAN INDIAN POPULATIONS: I & II. MSS Information Corporation, N.Y., (N.A.S. Library, U.C.B.).

American Indian Historical Society (1974), THE NATIVE AMERICAN TODAY, Indian Historian Press, San Francisco, (Issues on Ed., Water Rights, Land Use & Economy, Health Professions).

_____ (1970),INDIAN VOICES, THE FIRST CONVOCATION OF AMERICAN INDIAN SCHOLARS, The Indian Historian Press, San Francisco (Different topics: Philosophy, 1968 Civil Rights Act in Tribal Autonomy, Ed., Psychology and Child Development, etc.).

Anderson, Kenneth (1953), THE EDUCATIONAL ACHIEVEMENTS OF INDIAN CHILDREN, Bureau of Indian Affairs, Department of the Interior, Washington, DC.

Andrist, Ralph (1964), THE LONG DEATH, THE LAST DAYS OF THE PLAINS INDIANS, Collier-MacMillan Limited, London.

Atkinson, M. Jourdan (1935), INDIANS OF THE SOUTHWEST, The Naylor Co., San Antonio, Texas.

Baader, Ethel (1927), INDIAN PLAYMATES OF NAVAJO LAND, Friendship Press, N.Y.

Bahr, Donald (1975), PIMA & PAPAGO RITUAL ORATORY, The Indian Historian Press, San Francisco.

_____ (1974), PIMAN SHAMANISM & STAYING SICKNESS, The University of Arizona Press, Tucson, Arizona.

Bahr, Howard (1972), NATIVE AMERICANS TODAY: SOCIOLOGICAL PERSPECTIVES, Harper-Row Publishers, N.Y.

Bahti, Tom (1970), SOUTHWESTERN CEREMONIES, KC Publications.

Ballard, Louis (Spring 1969), "Cultural Differences: A Major Theme in Cultural Enrichment," The Indian Historian, Vol. 2, No. 1, p. 4-7.

Ballard, W.L. (1978), THE YUCHI GREEN CORN CEREMONIAL: FORM & MEANING, University of California, Los Angeles.

Barnouw, Victor (October 1950), ACCULTURATION & PERSONALITY AMONG THE WISCONSIN CHIPPEWA, American Anthropological Association, V. 52, #4, Part 2.

Barbeau, Marius, MEDICINE MEN ON THE NORTH PACIFIC COAST, Department of Northern Affairs & National Resources, National Museum of Canada, Bulletin #152, Series #42.

Barrett, S.A. (1953), MIWOK MATERIAL CULTURE, Yosemite Natural History Association, Inc., Yosemite National Park.

Barrett, S.A. (1978), THE WASHO INDIANS, AMS Press, N.Y.

Battiste, Marie (June 6, 1977), COGNITIVE IMPERIALISM: THE LAST STAGE OF CULTURAL IMPERIALISM, (N.A.S. Library, U.C.B.).

Bean, Lowell John (1972), MUKAT'S PEOPLE, THE CAHUILLA INDIANS OF SOUTHERN CALIFORNIA, University of California Press.

_____ (1976), Blackburn, Thomas, NATIVE CALIFORNIANS, Ballena Press, Ramona, California.

Beatty, Willard (1944), EDUCATION FOR ACTION: SELECTED ARTICLES FROM INDIAN EDUCATION 1936-43, A Publication of the Education Division, (N.A.S. Library, U.C.B.).

_____ (1953), EDUCATION FOR CULTURAL CHANGE, INDIAN EDUCATION 1944-51, U.S. Department of the Interior, (N.A.S. Library, U.C.B.).

Beck, Peggy (1977), THE SACRED WAYS OF KNOWLEDGE, SOURCES OF LIFE, Navajo Community College, Arizona, (N.A.S. Library, U.C.B.).

Beckwith, Paul, CUSTOMS OF THE DAKOTAHS, Smithsonian Annual Report, (N.A.S. Library U.C.B.).

Beiser, Morton (March 1974), "A Hazard to Mental Health, Indian Boarding Schools," AMERICAN JOURNAL OF PSYCHIATRY, Vol. 131, p. 305-306.

Bender, Ruth N. and Stala, Taylor J., (Spring 1977), "I Care Indian Children--A Real Enlightenment", INDIAN FOSTER PARENT ASSOCIATION, PROGRAM DEVELOPMENT GRANT, Spring 1977.

Benson, Henry (1970), LIFE AMONG THE CHOCTAW INDIANS, L. Swormstedt & A. Poe Publishers, Ohio.

Bergman, R.L. (1971), "Navajo Peyote Use: It's Apparent Safety," AMERICAN JOURNAL OF PSYCHIATRY, 128 (6): p. 695-699, (Mental Health Program, Indian Health Service, Public H.S., Window Rock, Arizona).

Biglin, James E. and Wilson, Jack (May 1972), "Parental Attitudes Toward Indian Education", JOURNAL OF AMERICAN INDIAN EDUCATION.

Blackburn, Thomas (1975), DECEMBER'S CHILD, A BOOK OF CHUMASH ORAL NARRATIVES, University of California Press.

Boas, Franz (1964), THE CENTRAL ESKIMO, University of Nebraska Press, Lincoln, Nebraska.

Brant, Charles (1969), THE LIFE OF A KIOWA APACHE INDIAN, Dover Publications, Inc., N.Y.

Braroe, N.W. (1965), "Reciprocal Exploitation in an Indian-White Community", SOUTHWESTERN JOURNAL OF ANTHROPOLOGY, 21 (2): p. 166-178.

Briggs, Jean (1968), EMOTIONAL EXPRESSION, Northern Science Research Group, Dept. of   Indian Affairs & Northern Development, (N.A.S. Library, U.C.B.).

Brink, Pamela J. (1982), SOME ASPECTS OF CHANGE IN NORTHERN PAIUTE CHILD REARING PRACTICES IN WESTERN NEVADA, University of California, L.A., (at San Francisco State University Library).

Brown, Dee (1970), BURY MY HEART AT WOUNDED KNEE, Bantam Books, Toronto, N.Y. London.

Brown, Vinson (1969), THE POMO INDIANS OF CALIFORNIA, Naturegraph Publishers, Healdsburg, California.

Brusa, Betty (1975), SALINAN INDIANS OF CALIFORNIA AND THEIR NEIGHBORS, Naturegraph Publishers, Healdsburg, California.

Bryde, S.J. (1966), THE SIOUX INDIAN STUDENT: A STUDY OF SCHOLASTIC FAILURE AND PERSONALITY CONFLICT, NIMH, (N.A.S. Library, U.C.B.).

Burnette, Robert (1974), THE ROAD TO WOUNDED KNEE, Bantam Books, N.Y.

Capps, Walter (1976), SEEING WITH A NATIVE EYE, Harper Forum Books, N.Y.

Chance, Norman (1966), THE ESKIMO OF NORTH ALASKA, Holt, Rinehart, & Winston, N.Y.

Colson, Elizabeth (1974), AUTOBIOGRAPHIES OF THREE POMO WOMEN, Archaeological Research Facility, University of California, Berkeley, (N.A.S. Library U.C.B.).

Conrotto, Eugene (1973), MIWOK MEANS PEOPLE, Valley Publishers, Fresno, CA.

Cook, Sherburne (1976), THE CONFLICT BETWEEN THE CALIFORNIA INDIAN & WHITE CIVILIZATION, University of California Press.

Curtis, Edward (1907), THE NORTH AMERICAN INDIAN, Johnson Reprint Corporation, N.Y., V. 1-20, Each volume contains different tribes.

Dahlber, Henry (1968), "Community and Social Service," JOURNAL OF AMERICAN INDIAN EDUCATION, Vol. VII, No. 3, p. 15-19.

Dale, Edward (1949), THE INDIANS OF THE SOUTHWEST, A CENTURY OF DEVELOPMENT UNDER THE U.S., University of Oklahoma Press, Norman, Oklahoma.

Danziger, Edmund (1978), THE CHIPPEWAS OF LAKE SUPERIOR, University of Oklahoma Press, Norman, Oklahoma.

Davis, James T. (1963), ABORIGINAL CALIFORNIA, THREE STUDIES IN CULTURE HISTORY, University of California, Berkeley.

Davis, Mary, (June 1961). "Adoptive Placement of American Indian Children with non-Indian Families, Part II, One Agency's Approach to the Indian Adoption Project," CHILD WELFARE, Vol. 40, p. 12-15.

D'Azevedo, Warren (August 1963), THE WASHO INDIANS OF CALIFORNIA & NEVADA, Anthropological Papers, #67, University of Utah Press, Salt Lake City.

_____ (1966), THE CURRENT STATUS OF ANTHROPOLOGICAL RESEARCH IN THE GREAT BASIN: 1964, Publications Office Desert Research Institute, Reno, Nevada.

Debo, Angie (1970), A HISTORY OF THE INDIANS OF THE UNITED STATES, University of Oklahoma Press, Norman, Oklahoma.

Degler, C.N. (1972), "Indians and Other Americans," COMMENTARY, 54 (5), p. 68-72, (Stanford University).

Deloria, Vine (1969), CUSTER DIED FOR YOUR SINS, Collier-MacMillan Limited, London.

Denig, Edwin (1967), INDIAN TRIBES OF THE UPPER MISSOURI, The Bureau of American Ethnology, 46th Annual Report.

Dennis, Wayne (1950), THE HOPI CHILD, John Wiley & Sons, Inc., N.Y.

Densmore, Frances (1970), CHIPPEWA CUSTOMS, Ross & Haines, Inc., Minneapolis, Minnesota.

Dimock, E. & Riegel, B., (1971), "Volunteering to Help Indians Help Themselves," CHILDREN 18 (1): p. 23-27, (Graduate School of Social Work, San Diego State).

Dizmang, L.H., Watson, J., May, P.A. & Bopp, J., (1974), "Adolescent Suicide at an Indian Reservation," AMERICAN JOURNAL OF ORTHOPSYCHIATRY, 44 (1) p. 43-49). (Dept. of Social Services, Adams County, Colorado, 10 Shoshonean Indians under 25 committed suicide).

Dlugokinski, Eric & Kramer, Lyn, (June 1974), "A System of Neglect: Indian Boarding Schools," AMERICAN JOURNAL OF PSYCHIATRY, Vol. 131, p. 670-673.

Doran, C.M., (1972), "Attitudes of 309 American Indian Women Toward Birth Control," HEALTH SERVICES REPORTS, 87 (7), p. 658-663, (School of Medicine, Yale University, New Haven, Conn.).

Dowling, J.H. (1968), "A Rural Indian Community in an Urban Setting," HUMAN ORGANIZATION, Vol. 50, No. 3, p. 236-240.

Downs, James F., (1966), THE TWO WORLDS OF THE WASHO, Holt, Rienhart, & Winston, N.Y.

Dozier, Edward (1966), HANO, A TEWA INDIAN COMMUNITY IN ARIZONA, CASE STUDIES IN CULTURAL ANTHROPOLOGY, Holt, Rinehart & Winston, N.Y.

Drechsel, Emanuel J., (1976), "Ha, Now Me Stomany That! A Summary of Pidginization and Creolization of North American Indian Languages," INTERNATIONAL JOURNAL OF THE SOCIOLOGY OF LANGUAGE, 7, p. 63-81.

Driver, Harold (1961), INDIANS OF NORTH AMERICA, The University of Chicago Press.

Driver, Harold E., James A. Kenny, Herschel C. Hudson & Ora May Engle (July 1972), "Statistical Classification of North American Indian Ethnic Units," ETHNOLOGY, 11, 3, p. 311-339.

Drucker, Philip (1965), CULTURES OF THE NORTH PACIFIC COAST, Chandler Publishing Co., San Francisco, California.

Dunning, R.W. (1959), SOCIAL & ECONOMIC CHANGE AMONG THE NORTHERN OJIBWA,   University of Toronto Press, Toronto, Canada.

Dyen, Isidore (1974), LEXICAL RECONSTRUCTION, THE CASE OF THE PROTO-ATHAPASKAN KINSHIP SYSTEM, Cambridge University Press, N.Y.

Eggan, Fred (1950), SOCIAL ORGANIZATION OF THE WESTERN PUEBLOS, University of Chicago Press, Chicago & London.

_____ (1964), THE AMERICAN INDIAN, Aldine Publishing Co., Chicago, Illinois.

_____ (1937), SOCIAL ANTHROPOLOGY OF NORTH AMERICAN TRIBES, The University of Chicago Press, Chicago & London.

_____ (1966), THE AMERICAN INDIAN, PERSPECTIVES FOR THE STUDY OF SOCIAL CHANGE, Aldine Publishing Co., Chicago.

Erdoes, Richard (1978), THE NATIVE AMERICANS: NAVAJOS, Sterling Publishing Co., Inc., N.Y.

Erikson, Erik (1950), CHILDHOOD & SOCIETY, W.W. Norton & CO., Inc., N.Y.

Fanshel, David (November 1964), "Indian Adoption Research Project," CHILD WELFARE, Vol. 43, p. 486.

Farb, Peter (1968), MAN'S RISE TO CIVILIZATION, Avon Publishers, N.Y.

Farris, Charles & Lorene (September 1976), "Indian Children: The Struggle for Survival," JOURNAL OF THE NATIONAL ASSOCIATION OF SOCIAL WORKERS, Vol. 21, p. 386-389.

Fearn, Leif (1967), "The Education of Indian Children: Reflections," JOURNAL OF AMERICAN INDIAN EDUCATION, Vol. VII, No. 1, p. 27-31.

Fenton, William, LONG-TERM TRENDS OF CHANGE AMONG THE IROQUOIS, Smithsonian Institute, Washington, DC.

Fey, Harold (1959), INDIANS & OTHER AMERICANS, TWO WAYS OF LIFE MEET, Harper & Row Publishers, N.Y.

Fisher, A.D. (1969), "White Rites Vs. Indian Rights," TRANSACTION, 7(1); p. 29-33, University of Alberta, Edmonton, Canada.

Fiske, Shirley (Fall 1977), School of Public Ad., Univ. of Southern California, L.A.) "Intertribal Perceptions: Navajo and Pan-Indianism," ETHOS, 5, 3, p. 358-375.

Fletcher, Alice (1972), THE OMAHA TRIBE, V. I & II, University of Nebraska Press, Lincoln, Nebraska.

Fontana, Bernard L. (1972), LOOK TO THE MOUNTAIN TOP, Gousha Publications, San Jose, California.

Forbes, Jack (1968), NATIVE AMERICANS OF CALIFORNIA & NEVADA, Naturegraph Publishers.

CHRONOLOGY OF NATIVE AMERICAN HISTORY, Oakland Unified School District, Community Relations, (N.A.S. Library, U.C.B.).

Foreman, Grant (1934), THE FIVE CIVILIZED TRIBES, University of Oklahoma Press.

Foster, Mary Le Cron (Winter 1974), "Deep Structure in Symbolic Anthropology," ETHOS, 2, 4, p. 334-355. (Cultural Values - Whites & Navajos).

French, Laurence A. (August 1979), (University of Nebraska, Lincoln) NATIVE AMERICAN PRISON SURVIVAL SCHOOLS (Sociological Abstracts).

Frisbie, Charlotte (1967), KINAADDA, A STUDY OF THE NAVAJO GIRL'S PUBERTY CEREMONY, Wesleyan University Press, Middletown, Conn.

Garbarino, Merwyn (1976), NATIVE AMERICAN HERITAGE, Little, Brown & Co., Boston and Toronto.

_____ (1970), "Seminole Girl", Transaction, 7 (4), P. 40-46.

Geiger, Maynard (1976), AS THE PADRES SAW THEM, CALIFORNIA INDIANS LIFE & CUSTOMS, Santa Barbara Mission Archive Library.

Giffen, Naomi (1930), THE ROLES OF MEN & WOMEN IN ESKIMO CULTURE, The University of Chicago Press, Chicago, Illinois.

Gilpin, Laura (1968), THE ENDURING NAVAJO, University of Texas Press, Austin & London.

Goddard, Pliny (1964), AMERICAN ARCHAEOLOGY & ETHNOLOGY, The University Press, Berkeley, California.

_____ (1976), INDIANS OF THE SOUTHWEST, Rio Grande Press, Inc., Glorietta, N.M.

Goldrank, Esther (1945), CHANGING CONFIGURATIONS IN THE SOCIAL ORGANIZATION OF A BLACKFOOT TRIBE DURING THE RESERVE PERIOD, University of Washington Press, Seattle/London.

Goodman, Mary Ellen (1970), THE CULTURE OF CHILDHOOD, Teachers College Press, Columbia University.

Graburn, Nelson (1969), ESKIMOS WITHOUT IGLOOS, Little, Brown & Co., Boston.

Graham, Patrick E. & Taylor, Judson H. (May 1969), "Reservation and Tribal Customs, History, and Language," JOURNAL OF AMERICAN INDIAN EDUCATION.

Grant, Blanche (1976), THE TAOS INDIANS, Rio Grande Press, Inc., Glorietta, N.M.

Green, Rayna (Fall 1975), "The Pocahontas Perplex: The Image of Indian Women in American Culture," THE MASSACHUSETTS REVIEW, 15, 4, p. 498-714.

Grinnell, George (1923), THE CHEYENNE INDIANS, HISTORY & WAYS OF LIFE, University of Nebraska Press, Lincoln, Nebraska.

_____ CHEYENNE WOMAN CUSTOMS, University of Nebraska Press, Lincoln, Nebraska.

_____ (1962), BLACKFOOT LODGE TALES, University of Nebraska Press, Lincoln/London.

Guillemin, Jeanne (1975), URBAN RENEGADES, Columbia University Press, N.Y.

Gundlach, James H. & E. Roberts Alden (Auburn Univ., AL) (1978), THE EFFECTS OF ACCULTURATION UPON NATIVE AMERICAN ECONOMIC WELL-BEING, Sociological Abstract.

Hammershlag, Carl A., (October 1973), "Indian Education: A Human Systems Analysis," AMERICAN JOURNAL OF PSYCHIATRY, Vol. 130, No. 10, p. 1098-1102.

Hanson, Wynne (Late Fall 1978), "Grief Counseling with Native Americans," WHITE CLOUD JOURNAL, Vol. 1, No. 2.

_____ (October 1980), "The Urban Indian Woman and Her Family," SOCIAL CASEWORK.

Heizer, R.F. (1971), THE CALIFORNIA INDIANS, University of California Press, Berkeley, L.A. & London.

Hertzberg, Hazel (1967), THE GREAT TREE & THE LONGHOUSE, THE CULTURE OF THE IROQUOIS, American Anthropological Association, (N.A.S. Library U.C.B.).

Hewitt, J.N.B., STATUS OF WOMAN IN IROQUOIS POLITICS BEFORE 1784, Bureau of American Ethnology, Smithsonian Institute, Washington, DC, (N.A.S. Library, U.C.B.).

Hicks, George L. (1973), "The Same North & South: Ethnicity and Change in Two American Indian Groups," PROCEEDINGS OF THE AMERICAN ETHNOLOGICAL SOCIETY, p. 75-94. (Establishing relations with whites).

Hilger, Inez (1977), CHIPPEWA CHILD LIFE & ITS CULTURAL BACKGROUND, Scholarly Press, Inc., Michigan.

_____ (1939), A SOCIAL STUDY OF ONE HUNDRED FIFTY CHIPPEWA INDIAN FAMILIES OF THE WHITE EARTH RESERVATION OF MINNESOTA (Dissertation, N.A.S. Library U.C.B.). Catholic University of American Press, Washington, DC.

Hodge, William (1969), THE ALBUQUERQUE NAVAJOS, The University of Arizona Press, Tucson, Arizona.

Hoebel, E. Adamson (1960), THE CHEYENNES, INDIANS OF THE GREAT PLAINS, Holt, Rinehart, & Winston, N.Y.

Howell, Norma (1970), "Potawatomi Pregnancy & Child Birth," M.A. Thesis, University of Kansas.

Hunter, John (1973), MEMOIRS OF A CAPTIVITY AMONG THE INDIANS OF NORTH AMERICA, Schocken Books, N.Y.

Jacobs, Sue-Ellen (1968), BERDACHE: A BRIEF REVIEW OF THE LITERATURE, Journal of the University of Colorado, V. 1, #1, (N.A.S. Library, U.C.B., about homosexuality).

James, Harry (1974), PAGES FROM HOPI HISTORY, The University of Arizona Press, Tucson, Arizona.

James, Wharton (1973), LEARNING FROM THE INDIANS, Running Press, Philadelphia, Pennsylvania.

Johnson, Edward (1975), WALKER RIVER PAIUTES, A TRIBAL HISTORY, University of Utah Printing Service, Salt Lake City, Utah.

Jones, Livingston (1914), A STUDY OF THE THLINGETS OF ALASKA, Fleming H. Revell Co., N.Y.

Josephy, Alvin (1968), THE INDIAN HERITAGE OF AMERICA, Bantam Books, N.Y.

Keller, Charles (E. Illinois Univ., Charleston) (1978), THE INDIAN RESERVATION: A TOTAL INSTITUTION, Sociological Abstract.

Kniffen, Fred (1940), AMERICAN ARCHAEOLOGY & ETHNOLOGY, V. 36, University of California Press, Berkeley.

Krause, Aurel (1956), THE TLINGIT INDIANS, University of Washington

Kroeber, A.L. (1953), HANDBOOK OF THE INDIANS OF CALIFORNIA, California Book Co., Ltd., Berkeley, CA.

Lowie, Robert (1917), NOTES ON THE SOCIAL ORGANIZATION & CUSTOMS OF THE MANDAN, HIDATSA, & CROW INDIANS, The American Museum of Natural History, V. XXI, Pt. 1, AMS Press.

_____ (1922), THE RELIGION OF THE CROW INDIANS, The American Museum of Natural History, V. XXV, Pt. 2, AMS Press.

_____ (1929, NOTES ON HOPI CLANS & KINSHIP, The American Museum of Natural History, V. XXX, Pt. VI, AMS Press.

_____ (1963), INDIANS OF THE PLAINS, Natural History Press, Garden City, N.Y.

Lurie, Nancy O., (1976), "The Willow-O-The-Wisp of Indian Unity," INDIAN HISTORIAN 9, (3), p. 19-24.

MacGregor, Gordon (1946), WARRIORS WITHOUT WEAPONS, A STUDY OF THE SOCIETY & PERSONALITY DEVELOPMENT OF THE PINE RIDGE SIOUX, The University of Chicago Press, Chicago/London.

Margolin, Malcolm (1978), THE OHLONE WAY, Heyday Books, Berkeley, California.

McFeat, Tom (1966), INDIANS OF THE NORTH PACIFIC COAST, University of Washington Press, Seattle, London.

McGee, W.J. (1973), THE SIOUX INDIANS, Sol Lewis, N.Y., (A Socio-Ethnological History).

Mails, Thomas (1974), THE PEOPLE CALLED APACHE, Prentice-Hall Inc., Englewood Cliffs, N.J.

_____ (1972), THE MYSTIC WARRIORS OF THE PLAINS, Doubleday & Co., Inc., N.Y.

MayHall, Mildred (1962), THE KIOWAS, University of Oklahoma Press, Norman, Oklahoma.

Maynard, Eileen (Winter 1974), "Growing Negative Image of the Anthropologist Among American Indians," HUMAN ORGANIZATION, 33, 4, p. 402-404.

Mead, Margaret (1932), THE CHANGING CULTURE OF AN INDIAN TRIBE, Capricorn Books, N.Y.

Merriam, C. Hart (1962), STUDIES OF CALIFORNIA INDIANS, University of California Press, Berkeley,/L.A..

Metcalf, Ann (June 1976), "From Schoolgirl to Mother: The Effects of Education on Navajo Women," SOCIAL PROBLEMS, 23, 5, p. 535-544.

Miller, Dorothy (1977), (9215 Walkefield Ave., Panorama City, CA 91402) NATIVE AMERICAN WOMEN: LEADERSHIP IMAGES. Sociological Abstracts.

Mogan, Lewis (1962), LEAGUE OF THE IROQUOIS, Corinth Books, N.Y.

_____ (1954), LEAGUE OF THE HO-DE-NO SAU-NEE, OR IROQUOIS, V. 1, Human Relations Area Files, New Haven, Conn.

Moriarty, James (1969), CHINIGCHINIX, AN INDIGENOUS CALIFORNIA INDIAN RELIGION, Southland Press Co., L.A.

Neumann, Thomas W. (1976), "The Physiological Consequences of Child-Rearing Among Creek, Chicasaw & Choctaw," ANTHROPOLOGICA, 18, 1, p. 3-14.

Nurge, Ethel (1970), THE MODERN SIOUX, SOCIAL SYSTEMS & RESERVATION CULTURE, University of Nebraska Press.

Oberg, Kalervo (1973), THE SOCIAL ECONOMY OF THE TLINGIT INDIANS, University of Washington Press, Seattle & London.

Opler, Morris (1941), AN APACHE LIFE-WAY, ECONOMIC, SOCIAL & RELIGIOUS, University of Chicago Press, Chicago, Illinois.

_____ (1946), CHILDHOOD & YOUTH IN JICARRILLA APACHE SOCIETY, Southwest Museum, L.A., (N.A.S. Library, U.C.B.).

Oswalt, Wendell (1966), THIS LAND WAS THEIRS, A STUDY OF THE NORTH AMERICAN INDIAN, John Wiley & Sons, Inc., N.Y.

Parker, Arthur (1968), PARKER ON THE IROQUOIS, Syracuse University Press, N.Y.

_____ (1926), THE HISTORY OF THE SENECA INDIANS, Ira J. Friedman, Inc., N.Y.

Parsons, Elsie Clews (October 1924), "Tewa Mothers & Children," NORTH AMERICAN ETHNOLOGY, (N.A.S. Library, U.C.B.).

Patterson, A. (1975), "Among Arizona Indians--Fewer Red Apples," INDIAN HISTORIAN, 8, (3): p. 26-31.

Powers, Stephen (1976), TRIBES OF CALIFORNIA, University of California Press, Berkeley/L.A./London.

Price, John (1978), NATIVE STUDIES, AMERICAN & CANADIAN INDIANS, McGraw-Hill Ryerson Limited, N.Y./Toronto.

Radin, Paul (1963), THE AUTOBIOGRAPHY OF A WINNEBAGO INDIAN (Lifeways, acculturation and the peyote cult), Dover Publications, Inc., N.Y.

_____ (1970), THE WINNEBAGO TRIBE, University of Nebraska Press, Lincoln/London.

Ray, Verne (1963), PRIMITIVE PRAGMATISTS, THE MODOC INDIANS OF NORTHERN CALIFORNIA, University of Washington Press, Seattle.

Ray, Verne (1939), CULTURAL RELATIONS IN THE PLATEAU OF NORTHWESTERN AMERICA, The Southwest Museum, L.A.

Reichard, Gladys A., (1969), SOCIAL LIFE OF THE NAVAJO INDIANS, AMS Press, N.Y.

Reid, John Phillip (1970), A LAW OF BLOOD, THE PRIMITIVE LAW OF THE CHEROKEE NATION, New York University Press, N.Y.

Ritzenhaler, Robert (1970), THE WOODLAND INDIANS, The Natural History Press, Garden City, N.Y.

Robinson, Doane (1974), A HISTORY OF THE DAKOTA OR SIOUX INDIANS, Ross & Haines, Inc., Minneapolis, Minn.

Robinson, Dorothy (1972), NAVAJO INDIANS TODAY, The Naylor Co., San Antonio Texas, 1972.

Rockwell, Wilson (1956), THE UTES, A FORGOTTEN PEOPLE, Sage Books, Denver.

Rohner, Ronald (1967), THE PEOPLE OF GILFORD: A CONTEMPORARY KWAKIUTL VILLAGE, National Museum of Canada, Bulletin 225, Dept. of the Secretary of State, (N.A.S. Library, U.C.B.).

Ruffing, Lorraine Turner (April 1976), "Navajo Economic Development Subject to Cultural Constraints," ECONOMIC DEVELOPMENT & CULTURAL CHANGE, 24, 3, p. 611-621.

Russell, Frank (1975), THE PIMA INDIANS, University of Arizona Press, Tucson, Arizona.

Saslow, Harry L. & Harrover, May J. (1968), "Research on Psychological Adjustment of Indian Youth," AMERICAN JOURNAL OF PSYCHIATRY, Vol. 125, No. 2.

Schlegel, A. (1973), "The Adolescent Socialization of the Hopi Girl," ETHNOLOGY, 12 (4), p.   449-462, 1973, University of Pittsburgh, PA.

Schleiffer, Hedwig (1973), SACRED NARCOTIC PLANTS OF THE NEW WORLD INDIANS, Hafner Press, Collier MacMillan, N.Y.

Schoolcraft, Henry (1884), THE INDIAN TRIBES OF THE UNITED STATES, V. 1-6, Part I & II History, Antiquities, Customs, Religions, Arts, etc., J.B. Lippincott & Co., London.

Searcy, Ann McElroy (Sept. 1965), CONTEMPORARY & TRADITIONAL PRAIRIE POTAWATOMI CHILD LIFE, Dept. of Anthropology, University of Kansas, Lawrence (N.A.S. Library, U.C.B.).

Sheps, Efraim (January 1970), "Indian Youth's Attitude Toward Non-Indian Patterns of Life," JOURNAL OF AMERICAN INDIAN EDUCATION.

Smithson, Carma Lee (1971), THE HAVASUPAI WOMAN, Anthropological Papers, University of Utah, Johnson Reprint Corp., N.Y./London, (N.A.S. Library, U.C.B.).

Sorkin, Alan L. (Fall 1976), "The Economic & Social Status of the American Indian, 1940-1970," JOURNAL OF NEGRO EDUCATION, 45, 4, p. 432-447.

Spang, Alonza (October 1965), "Counseling the Indian," JOURNAL OF AMERICAN INDIAN EDUCATION, Vol. 5, p. 11-12.

Spencer, Robert (1977), THE NATIVE AMERICANS, ETHNOLOGY & BACKGROUND OF THE NORTH AMERICAN INDIANS, Harper & Row Publishers, N.Y.

Spicer, Edward (1969), A SHORT HISTORY OF THE INDIANS OF THE UNITED STATES, D. Van Nostrand Co., N.Y./London.

_____ (1961), PERSPECTIVES IN AMERICAN INDIAN CULTURE CHANGE, University of Chicago Press, Chicago/London.

Spinden, Herbert J. (1964), THE NEZ PERCE INDIANS, American Anthropological Association, Kraus Reprint Corporation, N.Y.

Spindler, George D. & Louis S. (March 1978), "Identity, Militancy, and Cultural Congruence: The Menominee & Kainai," THE ANNALS OF THE AMERICAN ACADEMY OF POLITICAL & SOCIAL SCIENCE, p. 73-85, 436.

Spindler, Louise (February 1962), "Menomini Women & Culture Change," AMERICAN ANTHROPOLOGICAL ASSOCIATION, V. 64, #1, Pt. 2.

Spoehr, Alexander (1944), THE FLORIDA SEMINOLE CAMP (Extended Family), Anthropological Series, Field, Museum of Natural History 33, p. 121-150, (N.A.S. Library, U.C.B.).

Stanley, Sam & Robert K. Thomas (March 1978), "Current Demographic & Social Trends Among North American Indians," THE ANNALS OF THE AMERICAN ACADEMY OF POLITICAL AND SOCIAL SCIENCE, 436, p. 111-120.

Steiner, Stan (1968), THE NEW INDIANS, A Delta Book, N.Y.

Stern, Theodore (1966), THE KLAMATH TRIBE, A PEOPLE & THEIR RESERVATION, University of Washington Press, Seattle/London.

Strong, Emory (1969), STONE AGE IN THE GREAT BASIN, Binford & Mort, Publishers, Portland, Oregon.

Strong, William (1972), ABORIGINAL SOCIETY IN SOUTHERN CALIFORNIA, Malki Museum   Press, Morongo Indian Reservation, Banning, California, (N.A.S. Library, U.C.B.).

Swanton, John (1952), THE INDIAN TRIBES OF NORTH AMERICA, Smithsonian Institution Press, City of Washington, (N.A.S. Library, U.C.B.).

Swanton, John (1946), THE INDIANS OF THE SOUTHEASTERN UNITED STATES, Bureau of Ethnology, Bulletin 137, Washington, DC.

_____ (1931), SOURCE MATERIAL FOR THE SOCIAL & CEREMONIAL LIFE OF THE CHOCTAW INDIANS, Bureau of American Ethnology, Bulletin 103, Washington, DC.

Thompson, Bobby & John H. Peterson Jr. (1973), "Mississippi Choctaw Identity, Genesis & Change," PROCEEDINGS OF THE AMERICAN ETHNOLOGICAL SOCIETY, p. 179-196.

Thompson, Laura (1950), CULTURE IN CRISIS, A STUDY OF HOPI INDIANS, Russell & Russell, N.Y.

Trigger, Bruce (1969), THE HURON, (Their culture), Holt, Rinehart, & Winston, N.Y.

Underhill, Ruth (1945), INDIANS OF THE PACIFIC NORTHWEST, Education, Bureau of Indian Affairs, Washington, DC, (N.A.S. Library, U.C.B.).

_____ (1965), RED MAN'S RELIGION, University of Chicago Press, Chicago/London.

_____ (1956), THE NAVAJOS, University of Oklahoma Press, Norman, Oklahoma.

Unger, Steven (1977), THE DESTRUCTION OF AMERICAN INDIAN FAMILIES, Association on American Indian Affairs, N.Y., (N.A.S. Library, U.C.B.).

Waddell, Jack O. (1973), AMERICAN INDIAN URBANIZATION, Dept. of Sociology & Anthropology, Purdue University, (N.A.S. Library, U.C.B.).

Walker, Deward (1972), THE EMERGENT NATIVE AMERICANS, (Selected Topics), Little, Brown, & CO., Boston.

_____ (1978), INDIANS OF IDAHO, The University Press of Idaho, Moscow, Idaho.

Wallace, Anthony (1970), THE DEATH & REBIRTH OF THE SENECA, Alfred A Knopf, N.H.

Walsh, Gerald (1971), INDIANS IN TRANSITION, AN INQUIRY APPROACH, McClelland & Stewart Limited, Toronto.

Washburne, Heluiz (1940), LAND OF THE GOOD SHADOWS, The John Day Co., N.Y.

Waters, Frank (1963), BOOK OF THE HOPI, The Viking Press, N.Y.

Wax, Murray (1971), INDIAN AMERICANS, UNITY & DIVERSITY, Prentice-Hall, Inc., Englewood Cliffs, N.J.

Weigel, Lawrence E. (Fall 1976), "Pre-Contact Cultural Ecology of the Nongatl Indians of Northwest California," HUMBOLDT JOURNAL OF SOCIAL RELATIONS, 4, 1, p. 55-62.

Weppner, Robert S. (October 1972), "An Empirical Test of the Assimilation of a Migrant Group into an Urban Milieu," ANTHROPOLOGICAL QUARTERLY, 45, 4, p. 262-273.

Wetmore, Ruth (1975), FIRST ON THE LAND, John F. Blair Publisher, Winston-Salem, North Carolina.

White, Lynn (1968), "Assimilation of the Spokane Indians: On Reservation vs. Off Reservation Residence," Dissertation, Washington State University, (N.A.S. Library, U.C.B.).

Whitman, William (1937), THE OTO, AMS Press, N.Y.

Williams, Walter (1979), SOUTHEASTERN INDIANS, University of Georgia Press, Athens, Georgia.

Wissler, Clark (1950), THE AMERICAN INDIAN, AN INTRODUCTION TO THE ANTHROPOLOGY OF THE NEW WORLD, Peter Smith, N.Y.

_____ (1912), SOCIAL ORGANIZATION & RITUALISTIC CEREMONIES OF THE BLACKFOOT INDIANS, AMS Press Inc., N.Y.

Witherspoon, Gary (1975), NAVAJO KINSHIP & MARRIAGE, University of Chicago Press, Chicago/London.

Yinger, J. Milton & George Eaton (March 1978), "The Integration of Americans of Indian Descent," THE ANNALS OF THE AMERICAN ACADEMY OF POLITICAL & SOCIAL SCIENCE, 436, p. 137-151.

Zimmerman, Bill (1976), AIRLIFT TO WOUNDED KNEE, Swallow Press, Inc., Chicago.

**N.A.S. Library, U.C.B. means Native American Studies Library, University of California, Berkeley.

BIBLIOGRAPHY

Social Work Practice With American Indians

METHODS BIBLIOGRAPHY

Aberle, David, (1966), "The Peyote Religion Among the Navajo," Viking Fund Publications in Anthropology, #42, N.Y.: Wenner-Gren Foundation.

_____ (1957), NAVAJO & UTE PEYOTISM: A CHRONOLOGICAL & DISTRIBUTIONAL STUDY, University of Colorado Press, Boulder, Colorado.

Albon, Joan, "American Indian Relocation: Problems of Dependency & Management in the City," PHYLON, 26:362-371.

_____, "Adjustment of Relocated American Indian Children in the S.F. Bay Area: Social Interaction & Indian Identity," HUMAN ORGANIZATION, 24:296-304.

Adams, Richard C. (1904), THE ANCIENT RELIGION OF THE DELAWARE INDIANS & OBSERVATIONS & REFLECTIONS, The Law Reporter Printing Company, Washington, DC.

_____ (1906), HISTORY OF THE DELAWARE INDIANS, Government Printing Office, Washington, DC.

Albaugh, B.J. & Anderson, P.O. (Nov. 1974), "Peyote in the Treatment of Alcoholism Among American Indians," AMERICAN JOURNAL OF PSYCHIATRY, Vol. 131, No. 11, p. 1247-1255.

Alderfer, Clayton; Berk, David; Fisher, Scott; and Hammerschlag, Carl (1975), "Group Relations and the Expression of Aggression Among American Indian Tribes," SCHOOL OF ORGANIZATIONS AND MANAGEMENT, Yale University, New Haven.

Allinsmith, Wesley (1956), "Cultural Factors in Mental Health: An Anthropological Perspective," REVIEW OF EDUCATIONAL RESEARCH, 26 (5), P. 429-450.

American Indian Historical Society (1970), THE FIRST CONVOCATION OF AMERICAN INDIAN SCHOLARS, The Indian Historian Press, S.F. (Diff. Topics).

Ammon, Solomon (1975), HISTORY & PRESENT DEVELOPMENT OF INDIAN SCHOOLS IN THE UNITED STATES, R & E Research Associates, S.F., CA.

Archibald, Charles, Jr., (June 1971), "Mainstream--Where Indians Drown," HSMHA Health Reports, 86, V. 6, p. 489-494.

Attneave, Carolyn L. (November 1974), "Medicine Men and Psychiatrists in the Health Service", PSYCHIATRIC ANNUALS, 4:9, p. 49-55.

Baader, Ethel M. (1927), INDIAN PLAYMATES OF NAVAJO LAND, Friendship Press, N.Y.

Bach, John L. (October 1970), "New Indian War Against Suicide," TODAY'S HEALTH, Vol. 48, p. 16-17.

Bahr, Donald (1975), PIMA AND PAPAGO RITUAL ORATORY, The Indian Historian Press, S.F.

_____ (1974), PIMAN SHAMANISM & STAYING SICKNESS, The University of Arizona Press, Tucson, Arizona.

_____ (1973), "Psychiatry & Indian Curing," Indian Program, #2, p. 1-9.

Bahr, Howard (1972), NATIVE AMERICANS TODAY: SOCIOLOGICAL PERSPECTIVE, Harper & Row Publishers, N.Y.

Bahti, Tom (1970), SOUTHWESTERN INDIAN CEREMONIES, KC Publishers, Las Vegas Nevada.

Barbeau, Marius, MEDICINE MEN ON THE NORTH PACIFIC COAST, Dept. of Northern Affairs & National Resources, National Museum of Canada, Bulletin #152, Series #42.

Barnouw, Victor (October 1950), ACCULTURATION & PERSONALITY AMONG THE WISCONSIN CHIPPEWA, American Anthropological Association, V. 52, #4, Part 2.

Barter, Eloise (November 1974), "California Urban Indians and Mental Health Problems," PSYCHIATRIC ANNUALS, 4:9, p. 37-43.

Bassett, Dave (July 4, 1978), "Alcoholism and its impacts and responses in Industry," COMMUNITY RESOURCES, SWU 470.

Bean, John, & Wood, Corrinne (Fall 1969), "The Crisis in Indian Health: A California Example," THE INDIAN HISTORIAN, Vol. 2, No. 3.

Beck, Peggy (1977), THE SACRED WAYS OF KNOWLEDGE, SOURCES OF LIFE, Navajo Community College, Arizona.

Beiser, Morton (November 1974), "Body & Spirit Medicine: Conversations with a Navajo Singer," PSYCHIATRIC ANNUALS, 4:9, p. 10-12.

_____ (November 1974), "Indian Mental Health," PSYCHIATRIC ANNUALS, 4:9, p. 7-10.

_____ (November 1974), "The American Indian," PSYCHIATRIC ANNUALS, reprint, N.Y. Insight Communications, Inc.

_____ (March 1974), "A Hazard to Mental Health, Indian Boarding Schools," AMERICAN JOURNAL OF PSYCHIATRY, Vol. 131, p. 305-306.

Bennett, M.C. (1973), THE INDIAN COUNSELOR PROJECT HELP FOR THE ACCUSED, Canadian Journal of Criminology & Corrections, 15 (1): 1-6.

Bergman, R.L. (December 1971), "Navajo Peyote Use: Its Apparent Safety," AMERICAN JOURNAL OF PSYCHIATRY, Vol. 128, No. 6, p. 695-699.

_____ (July 1973), "Navajo Medicine and Psychoanalysis," HUMAN BEHAVIOR, p. 8-15.

Bergman, Robert L. (November 1974), "Paraprofessionals in Indian Health Programs," PSYCHIATRIC ANNUALS, 4:9, p. 76-84.

Blanchard, E.L. (May 1972), "Native American Lifeways and Their Implications for Social Work," presented at the NATIONAL CONFERENCE ON SOCIAL WELFARE, Chicago.

Boggs, Stephen T. (Feb. 1958), "Culture Change & the Personality of Ojibwa Children," AMERICAN ANTHROPOLOGIST 60, p. 47-58.

Bourke, John (1970), The Medicine Men of the Apache, Bureau of Ethnology, Government Printing Office, Washington, DC.

Boyer, Ruth M (June 1964), "The Matrifocal Family Among the Mescalero: Additional Data," AMERICAN ANTHROPOLOGIST 66, p. 593-602.

Braroe, N.W. (1965), RECIPROCAL EXPLOITATION IN AN INDIAN-WHITE COMMUNITY, SOUTHWESTERN JOURNAL OF ANTHROPOLOGY, 21 (2): 166-178.

Brockman, C. Thomas (1968), "The Social Classes at the Modern Flathead Indian Reservation," 8th Congress of Anthropological & Ethnological Sciences, p. 188-190.

Brown, E.F. (January 1977), "Indian Self-Determination: A Dilemma for Social Work Practice," in F.J. Pierce (Ed.) MENTAL HEALTH SERVICES AND SOCIAL WORK EDUCATION with Native Americans, Norman, Oklahoma, University of Oklahoma, School of Social Work.

Brown, Joseph (1972), THE SACRED PIPE, Penguin Books, Baltimore, Maryland.

_____ (1953), THE SPIRITUAL LEGACY OF THE AMERICAN INDIAN, University of Oklahoma Press, Norman, Oklahoma.

Brown, Vinson (1974), VOICES OF EARTH & SKY, VISION LIFE OF THE NATIVE AMERICANS, Stackpole Books.

Bryde, J.F. (1971), "Modern Indian Psychology, Vermillion, South Dakota: Institute of Indian Studies," University of South Dakota.

Bunzel, Ruth (1932), INTRODUCTION TO ZUNI CEREMONIALISM, 47th Annual Report of the Bureau of American Ethnology, Government Printing Office, Washington.

Burley, Sally (1958), "Some Factors Affecting the Adjustment of Relocated American Indians with Special References to the S.F.-Oakland Area, An Exploratory Survey," Master of Social Work Thesis, University of California.

Burnette, Robert (1974), THE ROAD TO WOUNDED KNEE, Bantam Books.

Campbell, Joseph (1970), MYTHS, DREAMS & RELIGION, E.P. Dutton & Co., In., N.Y.

Capps, Walter (1976), SEEING WITH A NATIVE EYE, ESSAYS ON NATIVE AMERICAN RELIGION, Harper & Row Books, N.Y.

Chadwick, B.A. & Stauss, J.H. (1975), THE ASSIMILATION OF AMERICAN INDIANS INTO URBAN SOCIETY: THE SEATTLE CASE, Human Organization 34, (4):359-69.

Chaudhuri, Joyotpaul (1974), URBAN INDIANS OF ARIZONA, PHOENIX, TUCSON, & FLAGSTAFF, University of Arizona Press, Tucson, Arizona.

Clifton, James A. (1961), KLAMATH PERSONALITIES: TEN RORSCHACH CASE STUDIES, University of Kansas, Lawrence, Kansas.

Cockerham, William C. & Audie L. Blevins, Jr. (Univ. of Illinois, Urbana & Univ. of Wyoming, Laramie) (April 1976), "Open School vs. Traditional School: Self-Identification Among Native Americans & White Adolescents," SOCIOLOGY OF EDUCATION, 49, 2, p. 164-169.

Collins, John James, (1967). "Peyotism & Religious Membership at Taos Pueblo, N.M.," THE SOUTHWESTERN SOCIAL SCIENCE QUARTERLY 48, p. 183-191.

Comstock, W.R. (April 1971). "On Seeing with the Eye of the Native European," Chap. 5, New York, 1976, CULTURAL CONFLICT IN URBAN INDIANS, by Joan Ablon, Ph.d.

Conrad, R.D. & Kahn, M.W. (January 1974), "An Epidemiological Study of Suicide and Attempted Suicide Among the Papago Indians," AMERICAN JOURNAL OF PSYCHIATRY, Vol. 131, No. 1, p. 69-72.

Corlett, William (1975). THE MEDICINE-MEN OF THE AMERICAN INDIAN & HIS CULTURAL BACKGROUND, Xerox University Microfilms, Ann Arbor, Michigan. (N.A.S. Library, U.C.B.).

Crompton, Don (June 1976). THE BIOGRAPHICAL INVENTORY AS A PREDICTIVE INSTRUMENT IN THE SELECTION OF INDIANS FOR TRAINING AS PARAPROFESSIONAL ALCOHOLISM COUNSELORS, Utah, DSW, (Univ. of Utah).

Curtis, Edward (1907). THE NORTH AMERICAN INDIAN, Johnson Reprint Corporation, N.Y., V. 1-20. Each volume contains different topics & tribes.

Deloria, Vine (1973). GOD IS RED, Grossett & Dunlap, N.Y.

DeMontigny, Lionel, (M.D.). "Doctor-Indian Patient Relationship," PORTLAND AREA INDIAN HEALTH SERVICE.

Devereux, George (1969). REALITY & DREAM, PSYCHOTHERAPY OF A PLAINS INDIAN, Doubleday & Co., Inc., Garden City, N.Y.

Dizmang, Larry H. (November 1974). "Suicide and the American Indian," PSYCHIATRIC ANNUALS, 4:9, p. 22-28.

_____, Watson, J., May, P.A. & Bopp, J. (1974). ADOLESCENT SUICIDE AT AN INDIAN RESERVATION, AMERICAN JOURNAL OF ORTHOPSYCHIATRY, 44(1), 43-49. Dept. of Social Services, Adams County, Colorado.

Dorsey, George (1971). THE CHEYENNE, I., CEREMONIAL ORGANIZATION, Rio Grande Press, Inc., Glorietta, N.M.

Dorsey, J. Owen (1970). OMAHA SOCIOLOGY, Bureau of Ethnology, Johnson Reprint Corporation, N.Y., London

Dozier, E.P. (1966). "Problem Drinking Among American Indians, The Role of Sociocultural Deprivation," QUARTERLY JOURNAL OF STUDIES OF ALCOHOL 27, #1, p. 72-87.

_____ (1966). A TEWA INDIAN COMMUNITY IN ARIZONA, CASE STUDIES IN CULTURAL ANTHROPOLOGY, Holt, Rinehart & Winston, N.Y.

Dran, Sandra, and David (May 1976). A COLLISION OF WORLD VIEWS: THEMES OF CULTURAL DIFFERENCES AND IMPLICATIONS FOR SOCIAL WORK WITH NATIVE AMERICANS, Masters Thesis, School of Social Work, Arizona State University.

Driver, Harold (1961). INDIANS OF NORTH AMERICA, The University of Chicago Press.

_____ James A. Kenny, Herschel C. Hudson & Ora May Engle, (Indiana University, Bloomington) (July 1972). STATISTICAL CLASSIFICATION OF NORTH AMERICAN ETHNIC UNITS, Ethnology, 11, 3, 311-339.

Dyer, D.T. (October 1969). "Human Problems in an Indian Culture," THE FAMILY COORDINATOR, p. 332-335.

Edwards, Dan (1975). "Too many whites and not enough human beings," Ethnicity: An Intervening variable in Social Word Education, from the JOURNAL OF EDUCATION.

Edwards, Eugene, D.A. (June 1976). DESCRIPTION OF EVALUATION OF AMERICAN INDIAN SOCIAL WORK TRAINING PROGRAMS, Utah D.S.W. (Four schools evaluated, Arizona S.U., Barry College of Florida, Univ. of Oklahoma, and Univ. of Utah).

Eliade, Mircea (1964). SHAMANISM, Princeton University Press.

Ellis, Richard (1972). THE WESTERN AMERICAN INDIAN, CASE STUDIES IN TRIBAL HISTORY, University of Nebraska Press, Lincoln.

Embree, Edwin (1939). INDIANS OF THE AMERICAS, Houghton Mifflin Co., Cambridge, Mass.

Ernst, Alice (1952). THE WOLF RITUAL OF THE NORTHWEST COAST, University of Oregon Press, Eugene, Oregon.

Etsitty, Clark (November 5, 1976), "Counseling the Navajo," SWU 478.

Everett, Michael (1971). "White Mountain Apache Medical Decision-Making," Chapter 11, in APACHEAN CULTURE HISTORY AND ETHNOLOGY, Edited by Keith Basso & Morris Opler, Anthropological papers, University of Arizona, 21, The University of Arizona Press.

Fanshe, David (1972). FAR FROM THE RESERVATION, (Adoption), Scarecrow Press, Inc., Metuchen, N.J.

Farris, C.E. (1976). "American Indian Social Work Advocates," SOCIAL CASEWORK, 57 (8): p. 494-503, School of Social Work, Barry College, Miami, Florida.

Fenton, William (1941). MASKED MEDICINE SOCIETIES OF THE IROQUOIS, Smithsonian Institute, Washington, DC.

Fergusson, Erna (1931). Dancing Gods, INDIAN CEREMONIALS OF NEW MEXICO AND ARIZONA, University of New Mexico Press, Albuquerque, NM.

_____ (Summer 1968). "Navajo Drinking: Some Tentative Hypothesis," HUMAN ORGANIZATION, Vo. 17, No. 2, p. 159-167.

Fewkes, Walter (1891). AMERICAN ETHNOLOGY AND ARCHAEOLOGY, V. 1-5, (Ceremonies on Different Tribes), The Riverside Press, Cambridge, MA.

_____ (1903). HOPI KATCHINAS AND CEREMONIES, Rio Grande Press, Inc., Glorieta, New Mexico.

Fields, S. (1976). "Folk Healing for the Wounded Spirit," INNOVATIONS, 3 (1); 2-18. (Navajo Medicine Men explains emotional, psychological, and behavioral problems).

Fine Day (1973). My Cree People, A TRIBAL HANDBOOK, GOOD MEDICINE BOOKS, V. 9, Calgary, Alberta.

Fields, D.B. (1970). THE ECONOMIC IMPACT OF THE PUBLIC SECTOR UPON THE INDIANS OF BRITISH COLUMBIA, University of British Columbia Press, Vancouver.

Fire, John Lame Deer (1972). LAME DEER, SEEKER OF VISIONS, A Touchstone Book., N.Y.

Fisher, A.D. (1969). "White Rites Vs. Indian Rights," TRANSACTION, 7(1): p. 29-33.

Fiske, Shirley (Fall 1977). (School of Public Ad., University of S. Cal. L.A.) "Intertribal Perceptions: Navajo and Pan-Indianism, ETHOS, 5, 3, p. 358-375.

Flannery, Regina & Cooper, John (1957). THE GROS VENTRES OF MONTANA: RELIGION & RITUAL, Catholic University of America Press, Washington, DC.

Fletcher, Alice (1915). INDIAN GAMES & DANCES WITH NATIVE SONGS, AMS Press, N.Y.

_____ (1972). THE OMAHA TRIBE, V. I & II, University of Nebraska Press, Lincoln, Nebraska.

Fontana, Bernard L. (1972). LOOK TO THE MOUNTAIN TOP, Gousha Publications, San Jose, California.

Forbes, Jack (1968). NATIVE AMERICANS OF CALIFORNIA & NEVADA, Naturegraph Publishers.

_____ (Jan. 1977). RELIGIOUS FREEDOM AND THE PROTECTION OF NATIVE AMERICAN PLACES OF WORSHIP AND CEMETERIES, University of California, Davis, California, (N.A.S. Library, U.C.B.).

Foster, Mary LeCron (1974). (Cal State Hayward) "Deep Structure in Symbolic Anthropology," ETHOS, 2, 4, Winter, p. 334-355, (Cultural values Whites & Navajos).

Foulks, Edward (1972). THE ARCTIC HYSTERIAS, American Anthropological Association Washington, DC (N.A.S. Library, U.C.B.).

Frisbie, Charlotte (1967). KINAADDA, A STUDY OF THE NAVAJA GIRLS'S PUBERTY CEREMONY, Wesleyan University Press, Middleton, Conn.

Fuchs, Michael (November 1975). "Use of Traditional Indian Medicine Among the Urban Native Americans," MEDICAL CARE, V. 13, #11.

Garbarino, Merwyn (1972). BIG CYPRESS, A CHANGING SEMINOLE COMMUNITY, Holt, Rinehart, & Winston, Inc., N.Y.

_____ (1976). NATIVE AMERICAN HERITAGE, Little, Brown, & Co., Boston and Toronto.

_____ (1970). "Seminole Girl," TRANSACTION, 7 (4): p. 40-46.

Geiger, Maynard (1976). AS THE PADRES SAW THEM, CALIFORNIA INDIANS LIFE & CUSTOMS, Santa Barbara Mission Archive Library.

Giffen, Naomi (1930). THE ROLES OF MEN & WOMEN IN ESKIMO CULTURE, The University Chicago Press, Chicago, Illinois.

Gill, Sam D. (Winter 1975). (Arizona State Univ., Tempe) "The Color of Navajo Ritual Symbolism: An Evaluation of Methods," JOURNAL OF ANTHROPOLOGICAL RESEARCH, 31, 4, p. 350-363.

Gilpin, Laura (1968). THE ENDURING NAVAJO, University of Texas Press, Austin & London.

Goddard, Pliny (1964). AMERICAN ARCHAEOLOGY & ETHNOLOGY, The University Press, Berkeley, California.

Gold, Delores, "Psychological Changes Associated with Acculturation of Saskatchewan Indians," JOURNAL OF SOCIAL PSYCHOLOGY, 71:177-184.

Goldfrank, Esther (1945). CHANGING CONFIGURATIONS IN THE SOCIAL ORGANIZATION OF A BLACKFOOT TRIBE DURING THE RESERVE PERIOD, University of Washington Press, Seattle/London.

Goldman (1975). THE MOUTH OF HEAVEN, (Kwakiutl Religious Thought), John Wiley & Sons, N.Y./London.

Gonzales, Patty Tolson (April 19, 1976). "A Paper comparing the alternative Health Care Delivery Systems of the Navajo Tribe and the Chicano/Puerto Rican Cultures," April 19, 1976, BEHAVIOR THE MINORITY EXPERIENCE.

Goodman, Mary Ellen (1970). THE CULTURE OF CHILDHOOD, Teachers College Press, Columbia University.

Graburn, Nelson (1969). ESKIMOS WITHOUT IGLOOS, Little, Brown & Co., Boston.

Graves, Theodore D., "The Personal Adjustment of Navajo Indian Migrants to Denver, Colorado," AMERICAN ANTHROPOLOGIST, 72:35-53.

_____, and Minor Van Arsdale, "Values, Expectations, and Relocation: The Navajo Migrant to Denver," HUMAN ORGANIZATION, 25:4, P. 300-307.

_____, (Fall 1973). "The Navajo Urban Migrant and His Psychological Situation", ETHOS, p. 321-334.

Graymont, Barbara (April 1969). THE TUSCARORA NEW YEAR FESTIVAL, New York History.

Green, Rayna (Fall 1975). (102 Trowbridge St., Apt. 5, Cambridge, Mass.) "The Pocahontas Perplex: The Image of Indian Women in American Culture," THE MASSACHUSETTS REVIEW,16, 4, p. 698-714.

Gundlach, James, & E. Roberts Alden (Auburn Univ., AL) THE EFFECTS OF ACCULTURATION UPON NATIVE AMERICAN ECONOMIC WELL-BEING.

Hallowell, A.I. (1967). "Study of the Acculturation & Personality of the Ojibwa," Chapter 18-20, CULTURE & EXPERIENCE, N.Y., Schocken Books.

Halpern, K.S. (1971). NAVAJO HEALTH & WELFARE AIDES: A FIELD STUDY, Social Service Review, 45(1), p. 37-52, (American Univ., Washington, DC).

Hammerschlag, C.A., Alderfer, C.P., & Berg, D. (1973). "Indian Education: A Human System Analysis," AMERICAN JOURNAL OF PSYCHIATRY, 130 (10), p. 1098-1102, (Indian Health Service, Phoenix, Arizona).

_____, "Identity Groups with American Indian Adolescents." (Unpublished paper).

Hammond, D. Corydon (Sept.-Oct., 1971). "Cross-Cultural Rehabilitation," JOURNAL OF REHABILITATION.

Hanson, Marshall R., (1960). "Plains Indians and Urbanization," Ph.D. Dissertation Dept. of Anthropology, Stanford, University (N.A.S. Library, U.C.B.).

Hanson, Wynne D. (1981). "Grief Counseling with Native Americans" in HUMAN SERVICES FOR CULTURAL MINORITIES Baltimore, University Park Press.

Hanson, Wynne DuBray (October 1980). "The Urban Indian Woman and her Family" in SOCIAL CASEWORK.

Havighurst, Robert (155). AMERICAN INDIAN & WHITE CHILDREN, University of Chicago Press, Chicago & London.

Hertzberg, Hazel W., (1971). "The Search for an American Indian Identity," Syracuse University Press.

Hicks, George L. (1973). (Brown Univ., Providence, RI) "The Same North & South: Ethnicity and Change in Two American Indian Groups," PROCEEDINGS OF THE AMERICAN ETHNOLOGICAL SOCIETY, P. 75-94.

Hilger, Inez (1939). A SOCIAL STUDY OF ONE HUNDRED FIFTY CHIPPEWA INDIAN FAMILIES OF THE WHITE EARTH RESERVATION OF MINNESOTA, (Dissertation, N.A.S. Library, U.C.B.) Catholic University of American Press, Washington, DC.

Hippler, Arthur E. (Spring 1974). Univ. of Alaska, Fairbanks). "Patterns of Sexual Behavior: The Athabascans of Interior Alaska," ETHOS, 2, 1, p. 47-68.

Hodge, William (1969). THE ALBUQUERQUE NAVAJOS, The University of Arizona Press, Tucson, Arizona.

Hoebel, E. Adamson (1960). THE CHEYENNES, INDIANS OF THE GREAT PLAINS, Holt, Rinehart & Winston, N.Y.

Hoffman, H. & Jackson, D.H., (1973). "Comparison of Measured Psychopathology in Indian and Non-Indian Alcoholics," PSYCHOLOGICAL REPORT, Vol. 33, p. 860-868.

Howard, James (Jan./Feb. 1967). THE PEYOTE RITUAL OF CHIEF WHITE BEAR, Museum News, University of South Dakota, V. 28, #1-2, (N.A.S. Library, U.C.B.).

Hultkrantz, Ake (1967). THE RELIGIONS OF THE AMERICAN INDIANS, University of California Press.

_____ (1976). "The Contribution of the Study of North American Indian Religions to the History of Religions," Chap. 7, in SEEING WITH A NATIVE EYE, Walter Capps, Harper & Row Publishers, N.Y.

Hundley, Norris (1974). THE AMERICAN INDIAN, Clio Books, Inc., Santa Barbara.

Hungry Wolf, Adolf (1977). THE BLOOD PEOPLE, A DIVISION OF THE BLACKFOOT CONFEDERACY, Harper & Row, Publishers, N.Y.

Hunter, John (1973). MEMOIRS OF A CAPTIVITY AMONG THE INDIANS OF NORTH AMERICA, Schocken Books, N.Y.

Hurt, Wesley, "The Urbanization of the Yankton Indians," HUMAN ORGANIZATION, 20:4, p. 226-231.

Hurt, Wesley, & Brown, R.M. (Fall 1965). "Social Drinking Patterns of the Yankton Sioux," HUMAN ORGANIZATION, 24, p. 22-230.

Jacobs, Sue-Ellen (1968). BERDACHE: A BRIEF REVIEW OF THE LITERATURE, Journal of the University of Colorado, V. 1, #1, (N.A.S. Library, U.C.B.).

Jensen, Gary F., Joseph H. Strauss, & V. William Harris, (Fall 1977). (Univ. of Arizona, Tucson) "Crime, Delinquency, and the American Indian," HUMAN ORGANIZATION, 36, 3, p. 252-257, (Alcohol-related offenses, tribal variations, economically disadvantaged backgrounds).

Jones, Dorothy M. (January, 1976). "The Mystique of Expertise in Social Services: An Alaska Example," JOURNAL OF SOCIOLOGY AND SOCIAL WELFARE, III, p. 332-346.

Jorgensen, Joseph (1972). THE SUN DANCE RELIGION, University of Chicago Press, Chicago/London.

Kadushin, Alfred (May 1972). "The Racial Factor in the Interview," SOCIAL WORK, Vol. 1, 7, Nov. 4, p. 88-89.

Kane, Robert (1972). FEDERAL HEALTH CARE, Springer Publishing Co., Inc., N.Y.

Karno, Marvin (1966). "The Enigma of Ethnicity in a Psychiatric Clinic," ARCHIVES OF GENERAL PSYCHIATRY, 14 (5): p. 516-520.

Keller, C. (1976). PRISON REFORM AND INDIANS, Indian Historian, 9(1), p. 34-38.

Keltner, Ron (June 1975). "A White Social worker on a Navajo Reservation: A Case Report of Culture Shock," unpublished paper.

Kiev, Ari (1964). MAGIC, FAITH, & HEALING, The Free Press, Collier MacMillan Publishers, N.Y.

King, Richard (1967). THE SCHOOL AT MOPASS, A PROBLEM OF IDENTITY, Holt, Rinehart & Winson, N.Y.

Kline, J.A. & Roberts, A.C., (1973). "A Residential Alcoholism Treatment Program for American Indians," QUARTERLY JOURNAL OF STUDIES ON ALCOHOL, Vol. 34, p. 860-868.

Kraus, Robert, "Suicidal Behavior in Four Native American Cultures," Research Precis, Xerox, (N.A.S. Library, U.C.B.).

_____ (1972). "A Psychoanalytic Interpretation of Shamanism," THE PSYCHOANALYTIC REVIEW 59, p. 19-32.

Krush, Thasseus, Bjork, John W., Sindell, Peter S., and Nelle, Joanne, (February 1966). "Some Thoughts on the Formation of Personality Disorder: Study of an Indian boarding School Population," AMERICAN JOURNAL OF PSYCHIATRY, Vol. 122, p. 868-876.

Kunitz, S.J., Levy, J.E., and Everett, M. (1970). "Alcoholic Cirrhosis Among the Navajo," QUARTERLY JOURNAL OF STUDIES ON ALCOHOL, Vol. 30, p. 672-685.

_____ Odoroff & J. Bollinger (Sept. 1971). (Univ. of Rochester School of Medicine, N.Y.) "The Epidemiology of Alcoholic Cirrhosis in Two Southwestern Indian Tribes," QUARTERLY JOURNAL OF STUDIES ON ALCOHOL, 32, 3, p. 706-720.

Kuttner, Robert E. & Lorincz, Albert B., Alcoholism and Addiction in Urbanized Sioux Indian.

LaBarre, Weston, (1959). THE PEYOTE CULT, Schocken Books, N.Y.

_____ (1962). THEY SHALL TAKE UP SERPENTS, PSYCHOLOGY OF THE SOUTHERN SNAKEHANDLING CULT, Schocken Books, N.Y.

Landes, Ruth (1971). THE OJIBWA WOMAN, W.W. Norton & Co., Inc., N.Y.

Lantis, Margaret (1947). ALASKAN ESKIMO CEREMONIALISM, J.J. Augustin Publisher, N.Y.

_____ (1960). ESKIMO CHILDHOOD & INTERPERSONAL RELATIONSHIPS, University Washington Press.

Leighton, Alexander (August 1968). "The Mental Health of the American Indian-Introduction" American Journal of Psychiatry 125, 113.

Leighton, Dorothea (1947). CHILDREN OF THE PEOPLE, Harvard University Press, Cambridge.

Leitka, Gene (October 1971). "Search for Identity creates Problems for Indian Students," JOURNAL OF AMERICAN INDIAN EDUCATION.

Levine, Stuart (1965). THE AMERICAN INDIAN TODAY, Penguin Books, Inc., Baltimore, Maryland.

Levy, Jerrold E. (Winter 1957). "Navajo Suicide" HUMAN ORGANIZATION 24, P. 308-318.

_____ (1974). INDIAN DRINKING, NAVAJO PRACTICES AND ANGL0-AMERICAN THEORIES, John Wiley & Sons, N.Y.

_____ (Summer 1969), Kunitz, S.J. & Everett, M., "Navajo Criminal Homicide," SOUTHWESTERN JOURNAL OF ANTHROPOLOGY p. 124-152.

_____ (Summer 1969), "Notes on Some White Mountain Apache Social Pathologies," PLATEAU 42, p. 11-19.

_____ (1971). "Indian Reservations, Anomie & Social Pathologies," SOUTHWESTERN JOURNAL OF ANTHROPOLOGY, 27 (2): p. 97-128. Portland State Univ.

Lewis, Ronald, & Ho, M.K. (1975). "Social Work with Native Americans," SOCIAL WORK 20, (5), P. 379-382, School of Social Work, Univ. of Oklahoma, Norman.

_____, "Tribal Social Worker--A Challenge to Creativity," J. Perice (ed.) MENTAL HEALTH SERVICES AND SOCIAL WORK EDUCATION WITH NATIVE AMERICANS, Norman, Oklahoma, Univ. of Oklahoma, School of Social Work.

Linquist, G.E. (1944). THE INDIAN IN AMERICAN LIFE, Friendship Press, N.Y.

Linton, Robert (1940). ACCULTURATION IN SEVEN AMERICAN INDIAN TRIBES, D. Appleton-Century Co., N.Y./London.

Littman, G. (Sept. 1970). "Alcoholism, Illness, and Social Pathology Among American Indians in Transition," AMERICAN JOURNAL OF PUBLIC HEALTH, Vol. 60, No. 9, p. 1769-1787.

Locklear, H.H., "American Indian Myths," SOCIAL WORK, Vol. 17, No. 3, p. 72-80.

_____ (1977). "American Indian Alcoholism: Program for Treatment," SOCIAL WORK, 22 (3), p. 202-207, (Baltimore City Dept. of Social Services, Baltimore, MD).

Lone Dog, Louise (1964). STRANGE JOURNEY, THE VISION LIFE OF A PSYCHIC INDIAN WOMAN, Naturegraph Publishers, Healdsburg, CA.

Luckert, Karl (1977). NAVAJO MOUNTAIN & RAINBOW BRIDGE RELIGION, The Museum of Northern Arizona, Flagstaff, Arizona.

_____ (1979). A NAVAJO HOLYWAY HEALING CEREMONIAL, University of Arizona Press, Tucson, Arizona.

Lurie, Nancy O., "Variant Adaptations of Minority Groups to Encompassing Systems," (Unpublished).

MacGregor, Gordon (1946). WARRIORS WITHOUT WEAPONS, A STUDY OF THE SOCIETY & PERSONALITY DEVELOPMENT OF THE PINE RIDGE SIOUX, The University of Chicago Press, Chicago/London.

McCone, R. Clyde (1968). "Death & the Persistence of Basic Personality Structure Among the Lakota," PLAINS ANTHROPOLOGIST 13, #42, Part 1, p. 305-309.

McFee, Malcolm, "The 150% Man, A Product of Blackfeet Acculturation," AMERICAN ANTHROPOLOGIST, 70:1096-1102.

McKenna, Margaret A. (Seattle Indian Health Board, 1131 14th Ave. S. WA) URBAN INDIAN ILLNESS BEHAVIOR: VACILLATING BETWEEN TWO CULTURAL REALMS.

McLeod, J. & Clark, S.A., (1974). "It's in the Blood?" CANADIAN WELFARE, 50 (5): 16-20, (Sociology Dept., Univ. of Saskatchewan, Saskatoon, Canada, Alcoholism, background & explanation, common cause-stress).

McNickle, Darcy (1973). NATIVE AMERICAN TRIBALISM, Oxford University Press, N.Y.

McSwain, Romola (1965). "The Role of Wives in the Urban Adjustment of Navajo Migrant Families to Denver, Colorado," Unpublished MA Thesis, University of Hawaii.

Maddox, John Lee (1923). THE MEDICINE MAN, MacMillan Col., N.Y.

Mail, Patricia (March 1978). (Seattle Univ., Washington). "Hippocrates Was a Medicine Man: The Health Care of Native Americans in the 20th Century," THE ANNALS OF THE AMERICAN ACADEMY OF POLITICAL & SOCIAL SCIENCE, 436, p. 40-49.

Mails, Thomas (1974). THE PEOPLE CALLED APACHE, Prentice-Hall Inc., Englewood Cliffs, N.J.

_____ (1972). THE MYSTIC WARRIORS OF THE PLAINS, Doubleday & Co., N.Y.

Malan, Vernon D. (1958). "The Dakota Indian Family, Community Studies on the Pine Ridge Reservation," Bulletin 470, Brookings: Rural Sociology Dept. South Dakota State College.

_____ (1959). "The Dakota Indian Religion," Bulletin 473, Brookings: South Dakota State College, Agricultural Experiment Station.

Marriott, Alice and Carol K. Racklin (1962). Urbanization Problems of Oklahoma Indians," Oklahoma Health and Welfare Association, Oklahoma City.

_____ (1968). AMERICAN INDIAN MYTHOLOGY, A Mentor Book, N.Y.

_____ (1975). PLAINS INDIAN MYTHOLOGY, Thomas Y. Crowell Co., N.Y.

Martin, Harry W., "Correlates of Adjustment Among American Indians in an Urban Environment," HUMAN ORGANIZATION, 23:4, p. 290-295.

Marty, Martin (Spring 1977). (Univ. of Chicago, Il.) "The Land & The City in American Religious Conflict," REVIEW OF RELIGIOUS RESEARCH, 18, 3, P. 211-232.

Matthews, Washington (1970). THE MOUNTAIN CHANT, A NAVAJO CEREMONY, Smithsonian Institute, Bureau of Ethnology, Washington, DC.

Mead, Margaret (1932). THE CHANGING CULTURE OF AN INDIAN TRIBE, Capricorn Books, N.Y.

Medicine, B. (1975). "The Role of Women in Native American Societies," a bibliography, INDIAN HISTORIAN, 8 (3), p. 50-54.

Meighan, Clement (1972). THE MARU CULT OF THE POMO CULTURE OF CALIFORNIA, GHOST DANCE SURVIVAL, Southwest Museum, Los Angeles.

Middleton, John (1967). MAGIC, WITCHCRAFT, AND CURING, The Natural History Press, Garde n City, N.Y.

Miller, Dorothy, L. (9215 Wakefield Ave., Panorama City, CA). NATIVE AMERICAN WOMEN: LEADERSHIP IMAGES.

Miller, Frank & Caulkins, D. Douglas, (Summer 1964). "Chippewa Adolescents: A Changing Generation," HUMAN ORGANIZATION 23, P. 150-159.

Milner, John G. (March 29, 1977). "American Indian and Anglo Considerations for Early Childhood Development," paper presented at the All Indian Foster Parent Conference held in Phoenix, Arizona.

Minnesota University Training Center for Community Programs (August 1970). PROBLEMS WITH ALCOHOL AMONG URBAN INDIANS IN MINNEAPOLIS (N.A.S. Library, U.C.B.).

_____ (July 1971). THE INDIAN CENTER (N.A.S. Library, U.C.B.).

_____ (July 1970). INDIANS OF THE URBAN SLUMS: FIELD NOTES FROM MINNEAPOLIS, (N.A.S. Library, U.C.B.).

_____ (Jan. 1970). RURAL & CITY INDIANS IN MINNESOTA PRISONS, (N.A.S. Library, U.C.B.).

_____ (July 1971). INTERRACIAL ASPECTS, (N.A.S. Library, U.C.B.).

Mooney, James (1965). THE GHOST-DANCE RELIGION & THE SIOUX OUTBREAK OF 1890, University of Chicago Press, Chicago/London.

Morey, Sylvester M. & Gilliam, Olivia L., "The Modern Indians Dilemma," Chapter 14, in RESPECT FOR LIFE, Waldorf Press, Adelphi University, Garden City, N.Y.

_____ (1970). CAN THE RED MAN HELP THE WHITE MAN, A DENVER CONFERENCE WITH INDIAN ELDERS, The Myrin Institute, Inc., N.Y., (N.A.S. Library, U.C.B.).

Morris, Robert (Sept. 1977). "Caring for VS Caring About People," SOCIAL WORK.

Moss, Fenton (1967). AN INDIAN ALCOHOLISM TRAINING PROJECT, University of Utah, Bureau of Indian Affairs, (N.A.S. Library, U.C.B.).

Moriarty, James (1969). CHINIGCHINIX, AN INDIGENOUS CALIFORNIA INDIAN RELIGION, Southland Press, Co., Los Angeles.

Nagler, Mark I. (1978). (Renison College Univ., Waterloo, Ontario). RED POWER AS A NATIONALISTIC MOVEMENT, Sociological Abstract.

_____ (1970). "Indians in the City," Canadian Research Center for Anthropology, St. Paul University, Ottawa.

"Navajo Psychotherapy," (June 12, 1972), TIME MAGAZINE.

Neihardt, John (1961). BLACK ELK SPEAKS, Bison Books, University of Nebraska.

Newcomb, Franc (1964). NAVAJO MEDICINE MAN & SAND PAINTER, University of Oklahoma Press, Norman, Oklahoma.

Nichols, Roger (1971). THE AMERICAN INDIAN: PAST AND PRESENT, John Wiley & Sons, Inc., N.Y.

Noyes, Francie (Sept. 28-Oct. 5, 1977). "Medicine Man Still Makes House Calls," NEW TIMES WEEKLY, Vol. 9, No. 30.

Opland, David V. (Winter 1977). "Marriage & Divorce for the Devils Lake Indian Reservations," N.D. LAW REVIEW, p. 317-334.

Opler, Morris (1941). AN APACHE LIFE-WAY, ECONOMIC, SOCIAL & RELIGIOUS, University of Chicago Press, Illinois.

Parker, Arthur. THE CODE OF HANDSOME LAKE, THE SENECA PROPHET, University of the State of N.Y., Education Dept., Bulletin 1912 (N.A.S. Library, U.C.B.).

Parkin, Michael (February 1974). (Suicide Prevention & Crisis Service, Buffalo, N.Y. 14202), "Suicide and Culture in Fairbanks: A Comparison of Three Cultural Groups in a Small City of Interior Alaska," PSYCHIATRY, 37, 1, p. 60-67.

Petrullo (1934). THE DIABOLIC ROOT, A STUDY OF PEYOTISM, THE NEW INDIAN RELIGION AMONG THE DELAWARES, University of Pennsylvania Press, Philadelphia, (N.A.S. Library, U.C.B.).

Ploacca, K. (Sept. 8, 1966). "Ways of Working with Navajos who have not learned the White Man's Ways," NAVAJO TIMES.

Powers, William (1975). OGLALA RELIGION, University of Nebraska Press, Lincoln/London.

Price, John A., "The Migration and Adaption of American Indians to Los Angeles," HUMAN ORGANIZATION, 27:2 P. 163-175.

_____ (1978). NATIVE STUDIES, AMERICAN & CANADIAN INDIANS, McGraw-Hill Ryerson Limited, N.Y./Toronto.

_____ (Spring 1975). "An Applied Analysis of North American Indians Drinking Patterns," HUMAN ORGANIZATION, Vol. 34, No. 1, p. 17-26.

Radin, Paul (1927). PRIMITIVE MAN AS PHILOSOPHER, Dover Publications, Inc., N.Y.

_____ (1945). THE ROAD OF LIFE & DEATH, Bollinger Series V, Patheon Books Inc., N.Y.

Reichard, Gladys (1950). NAVAJO RELIGION, A STUDY OF SYMBOLISM, Bollinger Series XVIII, Princetone University Press.

_____ (1928). SOCIAL LIFE OF THE NAVAJO INDIANS, AMS Press, N.Y.

Resnick, H.L. P., & Dizmang, L.H. (January 1971). "Observations on Suicidal Behavior Among American Indians," AMERICAN JOURNAL OF PSYCHIATRY, Vol. 127, No. 7, p. 882-887.

Robbins, R.H. (February 1973). "Alcohol & the Identity Struggle: Some Effects of Economic Change on Interpersonal Relations," AMERICAN ANTHROPOLOGIST 75, P. 99-122.

Robertson, G.G. & Baizerman, M. (1969). "Psychiatric Consultation on Two Indian Reservations," HOSPITAL & COMMUNITY PSYCHIATRY, 20, (6), 186, (Veterans Ad. Hospital, Sheridan, Wyoming).

Rohner, Ronald (1967). THE PEOPLE OF GILFORD: A CONTEMPORARY KWAKIUTL VILLAGE, National Museum of Canada, Bulletin 225, Dept. of the Secretary of State, (N.A.S. Library, U.C.B.).

Roos, Philip D., Dowell H. Smith & Stephen Langley (133 Summer St., Somerville, MA 02143), The Impact of AIM at Pine Ridge, (Sociological Abstract, SSSP Supplement #71).

Roy, C. (December 1970). "Prevalence of Mental Disorders Among Saskatchewan Indians," JOURNAL OF CROSS-CULTURAL PSYCHOLOGY, Vol. 1, No. 4, p. 383-392.

_____ (March 1973). "Indian Peyotists and Alcohol," AMERICAN JOURNAL OF PSYCHIATRY, Vol. 130, No. 3, p. 329-330.

Sandner, Donald (1979). NAVAJO SYMBOLS OF HEALING, Harcourt Brace Jovanovich, N.Y., London.

Saslow, Harry L. & Harrover, M.J. (1968). "Research on Psychological Adjustment of Indian Youth," AMERICAN JOURNAL OF PSYCHIATRY 125, #2, p. 224-231.

Schleiffer, Hedwig (1973). SACRED NARCOTIC PLANTS OF THE NEW WORLD INDIANS, Hafner Press, Collier, MacMillan, N.Y.

Schoolcraft, Henry (1884). THE INDIAN TRIBES OF THE UNITED STATES, V. 1-6, Part I & II History, Antiquities, Customs, Religion, Arts, Etc., J.B. Lippincott and Co., London.

Scientific Analysis (October 15, 1975). AMERICAN INDIAN SOCIALIZATION TO URBAN LIFE, Native American Research Group, NIMH, (N.A.S., Library, U.C.B.).

Searcy, Ann McElroy (Sept. 1965). CONTEMPORARY & TRADITIONAL PRAIRIES POTAWATOMI CHILD LIFE, Dept. of Anthropology, University of Kansas, Lawrence, (N.A.S. Library, U.C.B.).

Seton, Ernest (1966). THE GOSPEL OF THE REDMAN, AN INDIAN BIBLE, Seton Village, Santa Fe, N.M., (N.A.S. Library, U.C.B.).

Shore, James H. (November 1974). "Psychiatric Epidemiology Among American Indians," PSYCHIATRIC ANNALS, 4.9, The American Indian, P. 56-64.

_____ & Von Fumetti, B. (May 1972). "Three Alcohol Programs for American Indians," AMERICAN JOURNAL OF PSYCHIATRY, Vol. 128, N. 11, p. 1450-1454.

Sievers, M.L. (January 1968). "Cigarette and Alcohol Usage by Southwestern American Indians" AMERICAN JOURNAL OF PUBLIC HEALTH, Vol. 58, No. 1, p. 71-82.

Simmons, Robert (1942). SUN CHIEF, THE AUTOBIOGRAPHY OF A HOPI INDIAN, Yale University Press, New Haven/London.

Simpson, George (1957). "American Indians & American Life," THE ANNALS OF THE AMERICAN ACADEMY OF POLITICAL & SOCIAL SCIENCES, Philadelphia, (N.A.S. Library, U.C.B.).

Slotkin, J.S. (1956). THE PEYOTE RELIGION, A STUDY IN INDIAN-WHITE RELATIONS, The Free Press, Glencoe, Illinois.

Smith, David (1969). A STUDY OF THE RELATIONSHIP BETWEEN PARENTAL ATTITUDES OF NEZ PERCE INDIANS & THE ACHIEVEMENT OF THEIR CHILDREN, University Idaho, (N.A.S. Library, U.C.B.).

Social Service Dept., (February 1968). "Cultural Contrast" Indian Student Placement Service: Salt Lake City, Utah.

Spencer, Katherine (1957). AN ANALYSIS OF NAVAJO CHANTWAY MYTHS, American Folklore Society, Philadelphia.

Spang, A. (October 1965). "Counseling the Indian," JOURNAL OF AMERICAN INDIAN EDUCATION, Vol. 5, p. 11-12.

Spicer, Edward (1969). A SHORT HISTORY OF THE INDIANS OF THE UNITED STATES, D. Van Nostrand Co., N.Y./London.

_____ (1961). PERSPECTIVES IN AMERICAN INDIAN CULTURE CHANGE, University of Chicago Press, Chicago/London.

Spindler, George (1971). DREAMERS WITHOUT POWER, THE MENOMINI INDIANS, Holt, Rinehart & Winston, Inc., N.Y.

Spindler, George (1955). "Socio-Cultural & Psychological Processes in Menomini Acculturation," University of California Publications in Culture & Society, Berkeley, University of California Press.

Spindler, Louise (February 1962). AMERICAN ANTHROPOLOGICAL ASSOCIATION, V. 64, #1, Part 2.

Stage, Thomas B. & Keast, T.J. (1965). "A Psychiatric Service for Plains Indians" paper given at the 121st Annual Meeting of the American Psychiatric Association.

Stanley, Sam and Robert K. Thomas (March 1978). "Current Demographic & Social Trends Among North American Indians," THE ANNALS OF THE AMERICAN ACADEMY OF POLITICAL AND SOCIAL SCIENCE, 436, p. 111-120.

Steele, C. (1973). (Bake Univ., Baldwin City, KS) "Urban Indian Identity in Kansas: Some Implications for Research," PROCEEDINGS OF THE AMERICAN ETHNOLOGICAL SOCIETY, p. 167-178.

Steen, Shelia (1951). "The Psychological Consequences of Acculturation Among the Cape Breton Mimac."

Stewart, Omer (Sept. 1948). UTE PEYOTISM, A STUDY OF A CULTURAL COMPLEX, University of Colorado Press, (N.A.S. Library, U.C.B.).

_____ (Spring 1964). "Questions Regarding American Indian Criminality," HUMAN ORGANIZATION 23, p. 61-66.

Stone, Eric (1962). MEDICINE AMONG THE AMERICAN INDIANS, Hafner Publishing Co., N.Y.

Stratton, Ray, Zeiner, Arthur & Paredes, Alfonso (July 1978). "Tribal Affiliations & Prevalence of Alcohol Problems," JOURNAL OF STUDIES ON ALCOHOL, 39, 7, P. 1166-1177.

Straus, Anne S. (Fall 1977). "Northern Cheyenne Ethnopsychology" ETHOS, 5, 3, p. 326-357.

Stull, Donald D. (1973). "Modernization & Symptoms of Stress: Attitudes, Accidents and Alcohol Use Among Urban Papago Indians," Ph.D. Dissertation, University of Colorado, (N.A.S. Library, U.C.B.).

"Suicide Among the American Indians," (September 1967). NATIONAL INSTITUTE OF HEALTH.

Tax, Sol (March 1978). "The Impact of Urbanization on American Indians," THE ANNALS OF THE AMERICAN ACADEMY OF POLITICAL AND SOCIAL SCIENCE, 435, p. 121-136.

Teicher, Morton I. (1960). "Windigo Psychosis, A Study of a Relationship Between Belief and Behavior Among the Indians of Northeastern Canada," Proceedings, Annual Spring Meeting, Am. Ethnological Society, Univ. of Wash.

Thompson, Bobby & John H. Peterson Jr. (1973). "Mississippi Choctaw Identity: Genesis & Change," PROCEEDINGS OF THE AMERICAN ETHNOLOGICAL SOCIETY, p. 179-196.

Titiev, Mischa (1972). THE HOPE INDIANS OF OLD OLRAIBI, CHANGE & CONTINUITY, University of Michigan Press, Ann Arbor.

Tooker, Elisabeth (1970). THE IROQUOIS CEREMONIAL OF MIDWINTER, Syracuse University Press.

Torrey, E. Fuller (1974). COMMUNITY HEALTH & MENTAL HEALTH CARE DELIVERY FOR NORTH AMERICAN INDIANS, MSS Information Corporation, N.Y.

_____ (1970). "Mental Health Services for American Indians & Eskimos," COMMUNITY MENTAL HEALTH, 6 (6), p. 455-463, NIMH, Chevy Chase, MD.

TRAINING CENTER FOR COMMUNITY PROGRAMS, UNIVERSITY OF MINNESOTA.

Gregory, W. Craig, "Indian Housing in Minneapolis & St. Paul"

Drilling, Laverne, "The Indian Relief Recipient in Minneapolis"

Drilling, Vern, "Problems with Alcohol Among Urban Indians in Minneapolis"

Harkins, Arthur M., "Indian Americans in Dallas: Migrations, Missions, and Styles of Adaptation"

_____, "The Social Programs & Political Styles of Minneapolis Indians: an Interim Report"

_____, "Indian Americans in Duluth"

_____, "Attitudes of Minneapolis Agency Personnel Toward Urban Indians"

Trigger, Bruce (1969). THE HURON, THEIR CULTURE, Holt, Rinehart & Winston, N.Y.

Tyler, Hamilton (1964). PUEBLO GODS & MYTHS, University of Oklahoma Press, Norman.

Twiss, Gayla, "The Role of the Pipe in Dakota Religion."

Underhill, Ruth (1965). RED MAN'S RELIGION, University of Chicago Press London, Chicago.

_____ (1938). SINGING FOR POWER, University of California Press, Berkeley/L.A.

Unger, Steven (1977). THE DESTRUCTION OF AMERICAN INDIAN FAMILIES, Association on American Indian Affairs, N.Y., (N.A.S. Library, U.C.B.).

Valory, Dale Keith, YUROK DOCTORS & DEVILS: A STUDY IN IDENTITY, ANXIETY, AND DEVIANCE, Dissertation, Univ. of California, Berkeley, (N.A.S. Library, U.C.B.).

Vogel, Virgil, "American Indian Influences on: Medicine and Pharmacology" THE INDIAN HISTORIAN, Vol. 1.

_____ (1970). AMERICAN INDIAN MEDICINE, University of Oklahoma Press, Norman, Oklahoma.

Waddell, Jack O. (1971). THE AMERICAN INDIAN IN URBAN SOCIETY, Little, Brown, and Co.

_____ (Spring 1975). "For Individual Power and Social Credit: The Use of Alcohol among Tucson Papagos," HUMAN ORGANIZATION, Vol. 34, No. 1, p. 9-16.

_____ (1973). AMERICAN INDIAN URBANIZATION, Dept. of Sociology & Anthropology, Purdue University, (N.A.S. Library, U.C.B.).

Walker, Deward (1972). THE EMERGENT NATIVE AMERICANS, (Selected Topics), Little, Brown, & Co., Boston.

_____ (1968). CONFLICT & SCHISM IN NEZ PERCE ACCULTURATION, A STUDY OF RELIGION & POLITICS, Washington State University Press.

Wallace, Anthony (April 1958).   "Dreams & the Wishes of the Soul: A Type of Psychoanalytic Theory among the 17th Century Iroquois" Reprinted from American Anthropologist, V. 60, (N.A.S. LiBRARY, U.C.B.).

Walsh, Gerald (1971). INDIANS IN TRANSITION, AN INQUIRY APPROACH, McClelland & Stewart Limited, Toronto.

Water, Frank (1963). BOOK OF THE HOPI, The Viking Press, N.Y.

Wax, Murray, & Rosalie Was (March 1978). "Religion Among American Indians," THE ANNALS OF THE AMERICAN ACADEMY OF POLITICAL & SOCIAL SCIENCE, 436, 27-29.

Wax, Rosalie H. and Robert K. Thomas, "American Indians and White People" PHYLON, 22: 4 p. 305-317.

Weppner, Robert S. (October 1972). "An Empirical Test of the Assimilation of a Migrant Group into an Urban Milieu," ANTHROPOLOGICAL QUARTERLY, 45, 4, p. 262-273.

Westermeyer, J. (1972). "Options Regarding Alcohol Use Among the Chippewa," AMERICAN JOURNAL OF ORTHOPSYCHIATRY, 43 (3), p. 398-403.

Westfall, D.N. & Rosenbloom, A.L. (1971). "Diabetes Mellitus Among the Florida Seminoles," HSMHA HEALTH REPORTS, 86 (11), p. 1037-1041, (College of Medicine, University of Florida, Gainesville, Florida).

Wetmore, Ruth (1975). FIRST ON THE LAND, John F. Blair, Publisher, Winston-Salem, N.C.

"White Cloud Journal" of American Indian/Alaska Native Mental Health, V. 1, #1.

White Lynn (1968). ASSIMILATION OF THE SPOKANE INDIANS: ON RESERVATION VS. OFF RESERVATION RESIDENCE, Dissertation, Washington State Univ. (N.A.S. Library, U.C.B.).

White, R.A. (Sept. 1974). "Value Themes of the Native American Tribalistic Movement Among the South Dakota Sioux" CURRENT ANTHROPOLOGY, Vol. 15, No. 3, p. 284-303.

Whitman, William (1937). THE OTO, AMS Press, N.Y.

Wildschut, William (1975). CROW INDIAN MEDICINE BUNDLES, Museum of the American Indian, Heye Foundation, N.Y., (N.A.S. Library, U.C.B.).

Wilson, L.G. & Share, J.H. (1975). "Evaluation of a Regional Indian Alcohol Program," AMERICAN JOURNAL OF PSYCHIATRY, Vol. 132, p. 255-258.

Winkler, A.M. (1968). "Drinking on the American Frontier," QUARTERLY JOURNAL OF STUDIES ON ALCOHOL, Vol. 29, p. 413-445.

Wissler, Clark (1909). MYTHOLOGY OF THE BLACKFOOT INDIANS, American Museum of Natural History, V. II, Pt. 1, Order of the Trustee, N.Y.

_____ (1912). SOCIAL ORGANIZATION & RITUALISTIC CEREMONIES OF THE BLACKFOOT INDIANS, V. VII, 1912, Order of the Trustees, N.Y.

Wolf, Morris (1919). IROQUOIS RELIGION & IT'S RELATION TO THEIR MORALS, Dissertation, Columbia University Press, N.Y.

Wolfe, Andy, (Lincoln Indian Center, NE) INDIAN ALCOHOLISM.

Wolman, C. (1970). "Group Therapy in Two Languages, English and Navajo", AMERICAN JOURNAL OF PSYCHOTHERAPY, Vol. 24, p. 677-685.

Wright, Rolland (June 1972). THE AMERICAN INDIAN COLLEGE STUDENT: A STUDY IN MARGINALITY, Dissertation, Brandeis University, (N.A.S. Library, U.C.B.).

Wyman, Leland (1962). THE WINDWAYS OF THE NAVAJO, The Taylor Museum, Colorado Springs Fine Arts Center, 1962.

_____ (1970). BLESSINGWAY, University of Arizona Press, Tucson, Arizona.

Yarrow, H.C., (1880). STUDY OF MORTUARY CUSTOMS AMONG THE NORTH AMERICAN INDIANS, Government Printing Office, Washington, D.C., Smithsonian Institute.

Yinger, J. Milton, & George Eaton Simpson (March 1978). "The Integration of Americans of Indian Descent," THE ANNALS OF THE AMERICAN ACADEMY OF POLITICAL & SOCIAL SCIENCE, 436, p. 137-151.

INDEX

A

Aberle, 40
Ablon, 92
Accidents, 12
Adair, 41
Adoptions, 104
Albert, 38
Alcoholism, 12-13
Alienation, 52
Alstein, 104
Alkali Lake, 31
American Indians
    Agriculture, 2
    Architecture, 2
    Education, 8,10,22
    Employment, 10
    Population, 4
    Values, 33-48
    Women, 89
Anthropology, 47
Anasaza, 51
Apache, 40,47
Arapaho, 43
Arthur, 44

B

Balance, 51
Barry, 38
Being Orientation, 34,48
Benedict, 39
Bennett, 41
Bergman, 85,87
Blackfeet, 44,46
Bryde, 40,42
Burial Practices, 86
Bureau of Indian Affairs, 9, 14, 16

C

Casework, 61,66
Cherokee, 40,46,47
Chesky, 41
Child Welfare, 8, 103, 106
Chippewa, 46,47,96
Choctaw, 46
Client Centered, 82

G

Genocide, 1, 103
Gestalt, 78
Grants, 10
Green, 3
Grief, 72,84
Group Work, 82
Guilmet, 44
Gulick, 40,47

H

Hallowell, 40,93
Harmony with Nature, 51,57
Havighurst, 41
Healing, 76
Hidatsa, 46
Highschool, 3
Highwater, 51
Holistic Health, 75-76
Holzinger, 47
Homeless, 105
Homicide, 12
Honigmann, 40
Hopi, 40,46,47
Hughes, 51

I

Indian Child Welfare Act, 8, 111
Indian Health Service, 10,
Individualism, 49
Infant Mortality, 12
Iroquois,2,47,79

J

Jackson, 8
Johnson, 106
Johnson O'Malley Act, 8
Joseph, 41

K

Kaska, 40
Klamath, 2
Kluckhohn, 33,37,41,42,63
Kubler-Ross, 84,87